Here's what people are saying about Over the Rainbow:

This book is an absolute delight—filled with divine wisdom, spiritual insights, practical how-tos, and heart-radiating Love! It is filled with mystical, magical, and practical truths on every page. Your journey "over the rainbow" begins the moment you look at the cover and continues long after you read the last page. How you look at plants, gardens, nature, and Earth will forever be changed by a greater understanding of how we are all connected by water, soil, light, and Love! This book is truly a gift to Mother Earth and all Beings!
—Karen Cressman, spiritual interpreter, self-empowerment coach, author, and speaker

This radiant book is for all of us who have longed to have an ever more personal relationship to Earth through our garden. Tend to your plants with the deepening ability to sense that the tending is mutual. You are interacting with enormous Earth intelligence constantly offering you health and beauty through your garden. A single houseplant? A greenhouse to withstand freezing winters? A small plot? A little backyard refuge or a huge outside garden? It makes no difference. Do you long for the simple and profoundly renewing gift of interacting with Earth's timeless, generous, reciprocal nature? This amazing book will bring to you exactly the tools and strategies you need. Enrich the life of your garden and yourself simultaneously.
—Ellae Elinwood, *Transformation through Reflection* author, spiritual teacher, intuitive nature lover, gardener, and writer. Some of her books include *The Everything Numerology Book*, *Timeless Face*, and *Earth Is Your Sweet Spot*.

You don't have to be a gardener to find Marianne's *Over the Rainbow; A Gardener's Guide to Creating Light-Filled Gardens* one of the most delightful, enlightening, and inspiring books you'll ever read.

It is an exceptional guide to sowing and tending a garden, to be sure, but it also offers much more. It is a fount of knowledge about the plant, animal, and mineral kingdoms as well as the unseen devas, faeries, and other Nature beings who play essential roles in keeping our world healthy and humming. Love is the power that connects us with those myriad life forms.

Marianne explains how easy it is to converse with the animals and plants using what she calls the voice of the heart, and she recounts stories that show the intelligence and emotions of animals and plants to be similar to ours. I would say that their wisdom sometimes exceeds ours.

The illustrations in *Over the Rainbow* add enchantment to this treasure trove of gardening guidance and revelations about the other life-forms with whom we share this planet Earth.
—Suzanne Ward, author of *Amusing to Profound—My Conversations with Animals* and the *Matthew* book series

The book *Over the Rainbow; A Gardener's Guide to Creating Light-Filled Gardens* is a priceless gift of love and light for the entire world. It will profoundly inspire all who read it to find the joy of connecting to the Earth through the love they find in their own gardens.
—"The Wise Ones" (spoken through spiritual interpreter, Karen Cressman)

Once in a while, a book comes along at the perfect moment in time. *Over the Rainbow; A Gardener's Guide to Creating Light-Filled Gardens* is such a book. It is a must-read for gardeners, philosophers, lovers of literature, and cooks. It teaches without being pedantic and is chock-full of whimsy. It is a book written with a deep understanding of our Earth and the current condition of its creatures. It is a book infused with joy and great information, a veritable delight! I was moved by this book to eat healthier and to garden more wisely. I was reminded to be mindful and reverent of Nature's rhythms. Besides being refreshingly unique and inspiring, this book has the leitmotif of love! Love fosters beautiful gardens and creativity, the secret ingredient that the Earth rewards with abundance!
—Gigi Schaumburg, massage therapist, gardener, and social activist

I am a lifelong lover of nature. I met Marianne through a friend. The three of us danced, had dinner, and talked, discovering our mutual love of plants and animals. Later in my friendship with Marianne, I had the pleasure of seeing the vibrant garden of Marianne and her husband, Steve, in person. It was full of life, diversity, and beauty. The good energy was palpable. Later I was treated to a meal made from a medley of herbs, lettuces, and vegetables from their garden. It was delicious and positive proof that they walk their talk, with cooperation and inclusion of many aspects of Nature in their practical approach to gardening. Marianne's book has captured wonderful ways to develop your own beautiful garden.
—Deborah Smith, artist and energy-medicine practitioner

Over The Rainbow

Over The Rainbow

A Gardener's Guide To Creating Light-Filled Gardens

MARIANNE BRETTELL-VAUGHN WITH MARY TANNHEIMER

ISBN: 1542864356
ISBN-13: 9781542864350
Library of Congress Control Number: 2017901520
CreateSpace Independent Publishing Platform
North Charleston, South Carolina

For my mom and dad
and their tender hearts;
for my husband's smile,
my sister's laughter, and
my family's love;
for the Earth's 's beauty,
the garden's bounty,
and the Faeries' sparkle.
This book is for you.

Contents

Preface

Life begins the day you start a garden.

—Chinese proverb

Thank you, dear reader, for picking up this book. There's much to share about gardening here as well as about the many ways we can develop a deeper relationship with our planet, our Mother Earth.

We're in the midst of a momentous planetary change. All creatures of Nature, including us, are learning how to adapt to and evolve from these changes; thus, the gardening methods we've used in the past will also need to evolve and be adapted. It doesn't seem to matter where one lives on this spinning globe; everyone is affected by climate change. We have floods and droughts as well as excessive heat and polar-vortex cold to deal with, and we're figuring it out one day at a time. Many of us are evolving our social consciousness as well. We're becoming planetary activists and speaking up on behalf of the Earth. We're saying, "No more abuse!" That means we're saying no to the use of poisonous herbicides, deadly pesticides, chemical fertilizers, GMOs, and chemtrails. Each personal choice we make affects the whole.

This book provides insight and practical advice on some of the best choices we can make for the health of the planet and everyone on it. It is a call to love; it is time to embrace the truth that the Earth really *is* our Mother. Without the trees, we would not breathe; without the rivers, we would not drink; and without the plants and animals, we would not eat. It's that simple. Each of us will find our own unique way to move through our lives in a changing world. The purpose of this book is to help guide each of us to make conscious, loving choices in our gardens and in our lives. With this, we can make a difference in our world, and our beautiful planet will become the "Heaven on Earth" she was meant to be, one garden at a time.

1.

Part I
The Opening

One

Over the Rainbow

The garden is a love song, a duet between a human being and Mother Nature.

—Jeff Cox

*I*t's another blue-sky day in the garden. It's summertime and it's hot—at least 100°F—and I'm wilting. So is the garden. The drip system simply can't provide enough moisture for the garden vegetables in this heat, especially for the tall heirloom tomatoes, so I'm using the hose to cool them down. The plants are over four feet tall, and that's a lot of foliage to keep cool in the hot desert sun. "What to do?" I ask the garden. I notice a whisper in my heart, a familiar voice to me that says, "Sing to us!"

"What shall I sing?" I ask. I feel a smile in my heart as I "know" the answer, and I begin to sing. It's a childhood favorite that takes me above the clouds and into a beautiful new world. With the words of the song, the garden and I are no longer in the heat; we're "over the rainbow," where the sky is still electric blue, but somehow it doesn't feel so intense anymore. We're transported to another place where we feel refreshed and alive, and I just keep singing.

As I sing, I lovingly caress the tomato leaves, visualizing strength and vitality moving down the stems of each plant and going deep into their roots. I can feel them smiling, and as I continue to sing, I realize the whole garden is smiling and singing along with me. The flowers, the bees, and the birds—we're all "over the rainbow," and the feeling is amazing! From that day forward, together we continue to sing the rainbow song, and the three tomato plants (that I now lovingly call "the rainbow girls") provide us with beautiful fruit all summer long. In fact, the entire garden continues to shine, despite the heat, because we keep on traveling over the rainbow! It's a beautiful thing indeed.

> *If happy little faeries fly*
> *beyond the rainbow,*
> *why then, I can fly!*

Two

IT STARTS WITH THE HEART

So, how does one open up and hear that whisper in the heart?
...have a conversation with the garden,
...talk to nature while you walk through
the woods...or the park...
...or move through your own backyard?

It starts with the heart and the reawakening of the natural ability to connect that we're all born with. As children, we have a deep resonance with nature. But the "big people" in our lives usually convince us otherwise. They tell us that the faeries we see aren't real, that the shining colors we see around trees and plants are make-believe, and that the "little people" peeking out at us from behind the flowers are just "our imagination." But with love and a belief in ourselves, we can open that connection once again and bring the magic back into our lives.

The connection begins as we listen to the voice of the heart, which is our intuition. Our intuition speaks the truth, although it often gets drowned out by a louder voice, the voice of the rational mind. The rational mind leads us down the path of reason and logic, but this path doesn't always lead us to our highest truths. The path of the heart, which is neither reasonable nor logical, will always lead us there; we just need to listen.

When we use our hearts to speak with nature, we connect on a much deeper level. Because of this, we often discover more about the lives—and the feelings—of those plants and animals we're connecting with. The following story is a perfect example of this. It's a story about a pinyon pine tree and how, through connecting with that tree, I learned more than I ever thought possible. It was quite the eye-opening experience for me!

The pinyon pine lives along a trail in a canyon by my house, and I often hike and visit the tree. One spring, I noticed that the tree was stressed from another winter of drought. A few of its branches had died back, so I put my hands on the trunk of the tree and sent it lots of love. I never had the opportunity to visit the tree again that spring, and before I knew it, there was summer. It was just too hot to hike that trail in the summertime, so I didn't get a chance to visit the tree until the weather had cooled down in the fall. I was anxious to visit my tree friend again, and I was wondering how it was doing after another hot summer. Imagine my surprise when I found the tree was looking pretty healthy! No new branches had died back, and in fact, it had fresh green growth and new pinecones. We had received some monsoon moisture over the Sierras and into our valley over the summer, so I assumed that was why the tree looked healthy. But the Pinyon "told" me it wasn't just the rains that had given it the boost; it was the "rainbow" song. I couldn't believe it! The tree explained that plants and trees connect and communicate through their root systems in the Earth, and as I sang "Over the Rainbow" with love and compassion to my garden down below, the feelings reverberated through the Earth and touched the tree (who was already connected to me) way up the canyon. The tree continued to "listen in" and stay connected to the garden throughout the summer, and it enjoyed the rainbow song most of all. What a revelation for me!

A little while after I visited the tree, my friend Mary and I were out in the garden talking about how cool it was that singing "Over the Rainbow" had helped the garden so much. Mary then noticed the pinyon's energy stretching down to listen in, like a big arch bending over from the canyon above, almost in the shape of a rainbow, curiosity bristling from every branch. The tree was listening in with its "tree ears" so as not to miss a thing we were saying. We had to laugh at the image of the tree as it "bent down" to be with us way down in the garden.

I'm always amazed at how much awareness nature has about things—just like that Pinyon Pine tree—and I'm forever grateful for the wonderful communications we share and how much I learn from nature every day. So, now it's time for you to learn this "heart language" and experience your own communications with nature. Life will never be the same—I promise you that; it will only get better and better. So let the journey begin.

Three

The Communication Begins

All of nature is ready and willing to talk to you. You just need to relax, open your heart, and begin the conversation. It takes time to develop this skill, but with continued practice you'll get better at it.

To begin, we'll choose a plant for you to connect with. It can be a houseplant, a plant in the garden, or a plant out in nature. Choose a time for the following exercise when you won't be disturbed. Have a pen and paper (or a tablet) handy to record your questions and any responses you might receive from your plant or from nature.

Sit quietly for a few moments and breathe slowly and mindfully. Let go of the day and its concerns. Close your eyes (if they're not already) and put a hand on your heart, or, if that isn't your style, just focus on your heart. "Hold" your heart gently as you breathe slowly, consciously feeling the love that is in your heart. That is you; that is the love that you are. Feel the love, and let it fill your whole being. Sit with this for a moment, just feeling the love. You might feel warm, tingly, or happy inside. Just feel what you feel and keep breathing, slowly and mindfully. When you're ready, focus on the plant you've chosen to talk to, and bathe the plant in your love. Shower it with kindness and appreciation. Say hello through this heart connection and see if you "hear" or "feel" a response. Just stay open to any and all possibilities. For instance, you might "see" an image from the plant in your mind's eye, which is clairvoyance, or you might "hear" a message from the plant, which is clairaudience. Or, you might "feel" a sensation coming from the plant, which is clairsentience. Don't question the validity of the response. Just feel what you feel.

Once you've said hello, you can continue your conversation with the plant. You can speak either verbally or nonverbally, whichever you feel the most comfortable with. The plant will hear you. A good place to start might be to tell the plant how beautiful it is and that you admire its shape, its color, and maybe its fragrance too, if it has one. You could also tell the plant how happy you are to be having a conversation with it and ask whether it has anything special to share with you. Listen for any response you might receive from the plant. Do you hear a thank-you? Do you feel the plant "tingling" in response to your interest and admiration? Does it send love back to you? Now ask the plant a few simple questions about its life. Is it a happy plant? Does it receive enough light? Water? Nourishment? Love? Of course, these are just suggestions for you. Know that whatever conversation calls to you will be a perfect place for you to start. Remember to write down any response you receive from the plant, keeping in mind that simple yes-or-no answers are just as good as long ones. The most important thing is not to censor anything; just stay open, trust yourself, and know that the answers you receive are valid. Once you feel complete with all the questions you have for the plant, see if it has a special closing message for you. (They often do.) Stay open to the pictures, words, or feelings you receive and write them down. Say thank you to the plant, showering it with love and appreciation once more, and say good-bye. Sit in this space for a moment or two, feeling the love you just shared with the plant. Perhaps in the conversation you saw an image of a happy plant or heard the plant say hello to you. Or maybe you felt warmth and happiness, as though the plant was giving you a great big hug. We each have our own way of speaking, so however you received the messages, it was perfect for you. Know that the experience was real and you can trust it. But what if you didn't receive a response you could recognize? Just relax and trust the process, knowing that placing your hand on your heart or focusing there and saying hello with love is enough. It opens the communication channels, and with practice, you'll eventually receive a response. It's like toning a muscle that hasn't been used. It takes time for the muscle to develop, but with persistent training, it becomes almost effortless to use. Remember that you're toning your communication muscles, and they'll get stronger and more clear as you continue to use them. You'll find much joy as you begin to talk with the many realms of nature. You can talk not only to the plants and animals but also to the mountains, rivers, rocks, devas, faeries, and anyone else you're drawn to. They all have spirit, feeling, and a voice. The possibilities for communication—especially in the garden—are endless. You can ask questions about the care of your garden and receive a helpful response from the many beings that live there. You might get an intuitive "hit"—or message—concerning the needs of an individual plant or maybe the needs of your garden as a whole. You'll find it helpful to receive your garden information this way, as it comes straight from the source. Consider the experience I had in the garden when I asked nature what to do for those struggling tomatoes. The answer was to "sing to the garden," and so I did. The garden and I both benefitted greatly from the experience.

We are moving out of an age—the Piscean age—in which nature communication was not an accepted practice except among indigenous cultures. Now that we're moving into the Aquarian age, which signifies cooperation and communication, it's the perfect time to embrace a cocreative approach to life; learning how to communicate with the garden is a perfect place to start. We're setting the template for a whole new way of being on the Earth, and eventually this way will become the norm. So, let this new way and this new day begin where the story always begins—in the garden.

Four

LET'S TALK TO THE GARDEN

It is your state
that the nature
world responds to—not what you say,
not what you do, but who you are.

—The Devas

It's now time to be with your garden in a brand-new way—a way that embraces cocreativity, communication, and love. With love, all things are possible, and this includes the ability to talk to your garden and to have your garden talk back to you. So, let's go out into the garden and say hello! It doesn't matter whether your garden consists of a few pots on a balcony or a huge plot of land; the goal is to develop a new way of relating to your garden, no matter how big or small it is.

Sit quietly, close your eyes, and relax your breath. Place your hand on your heart, feeling the love that is there. (If you're not comfortable with this, just focus on your heart instead; that will work just fine.) Fill your whole body with love—a love that makes you smile—and send it out into the garden. Feel the love as it moves through the garden. Sit with it for a moment or two, just feeling the love. Then begin by saying hello. Do you hear a hello coming back to you? Does the hello make you smile? Next, say out loud or silently—the garden will hear you either way—that you're ready to begin a cocreative partnership with all members of the garden, which includes the plants, animals, trees, rocks, faeries, nature spirits, and devas. (If you're not sure about these various nature beings, just stay open to the possibility that they exist.) Let everyone know that your intention is to create a garden filled with love. Sit quietly and see if you get a response. Is the garden grateful that you've embraced a cocreative approach? Do you hear a thank-you from everyone in the garden? Does it make you smile? Whatever you receive is perfect. Sit with this for a moment, and feel the heart connection between you and your garden. Breathe in the love that is there, knowing that with practice it will keep getting better.

Now it's time to connect with the various members of the garden. This will give you the opportunity to develop personal relationships as you open up the lines of communication between you and all the beings that call the garden their home. To practice cocreativity in your garden, it's important to communicate with the garden in whatever way works for you. Once you've learned how to talk to your garden and received a response, you and the garden become true partners, and what you can create is so much richer than what you've created in the past. We are beginning a conversation here, and although there will be challenges in the garden from time to time—as we're all evolving, gardens and gardeners alike—you'll find the challenges easier to move through as the connections you've made continue to deepen.

Give yourself some time to do this process (about twenty minutes or so), as you're making new friends in the garden, and that takes time to develop. Once the process is complete, the connections will be in place, and it will be easy to communicate anytime you desire.

We'll begin by connecting with the insects in your garden. Sit quietly, hand on your heart, and fill yourself with love. Send the love out to all the insects that are there—the bees, butterflies, moths, ants, beetles, crickets, spiders, worms, slugs, snails, wasps, grasshoppers—*everyone* who lives there, not just the ones you like. Say hello, and see if you get a response. Many insects have experienced such an intense degree of hostility from us that when one of us actually sends them love, they're not quite sure what to do with it! It's hard to trust it, as the feeling is so new. So, if you don't receive a response right away, just keep sending them your love. Eventually they'll warm up to you and give you a response. What do you feel from them? Do you hear a hello? Do you feel a sense of gratitude as you send them your love? Do they seem happy to talk to you? If so, does the connection make you smile? Sit with this for a moment, and then ask if they have a message for you. You might see, feel, or sense a particular insect coming forward to greet you. Perhaps it's a butterfly with a message of love and lightheartedness. Or maybe it's a honeybee with a more urgent message, reminding you—and all of us—to treat the bees and the Earth with loving kindness and respect. Whoever comes forward with a message is perfect, and you can trust that. Say thank you to all the insects in the garden, and as you say good-bye, let them know you'll be connecting with them again.

Next, we'll connect with the animals in your garden. This includes the animals that you see in the daytime as well as those that visit at night. Say hello to the birds, squirrels, rabbits, lizards, frogs, snakes, skunks, mice, raccoons, deer, and anyone else you can think of. With your hand on your heart, send them love, and see whether you get a response. You might receive a welcoming hello from the animals as a group, or you might hear from an individual animal in the garden. If that's the case, see who has come forward to speak with you. Maybe it's a lizard, as they are usually quite curious and chatty. Or maybe it's a deer—they speak with gentleness and love. Or maybe it's a mouse, reminding you to honor him in the same way you do the other members of the garden. All animals, no matter how small, play an important role in the cycles of life. Whoever has brought you a message is perfect, so say thank you to that animal for its response. Let all the animals in your garden know that you're embracing a whole new way of being in the garden, one that practices inclusion instead of exclusion, and that all are welcome there. Ask them to help you to create a balanced garden in which their needs and your needs are met and everyone benefits. Sit quietly and see whether you get a response from the animals. Chances are you will, as they will be grateful for your open heart. Ask whether they have a closing message for you, and see who responds. Embrace whatever message you receive—whether you see it, hear it, or feel it—and say thank you to the animal. Send all the animals your love once more, letting them know you'll be connecting with them again.

Next, we'll move onto the plant realm, which includes the trees, bushes, grasses, flowers, vegetables, and herbs. With your hand on your heart, say hello and send your love to all the green members of your garden. Sit quietly, and see whether you receive a response. You will probably get a BIG hello from everyone in the garden, and then maybe a particular plant member will step forward to give you a message from the group. So, who wishes to speak with you today? Is it a tree in your garden, a flower, or maybe one of your beautiful herbs?

The plant world is so connected to us that when given the chance, they'll share lengthy and insightful information, which is always interesting and helpful. Whatever response you receive, take it to heart and say thank you. Let them know that your intention is to create a peaceful garden in which all the plants unfold in their own time, connecting with the pulse of the Earth. Tell them there will never be any chemical fertilizers used in the garden, as you know it pushes them to perform out of sync with the Earth. Tell them that instead they'll be given the opportunity to grow, bloom, and evolve within their own natural rhythms. Sit quietly and feel their response. No doubt you'll be showered with love from all the plants in your garden. Just take it in with a smile and say thank you, sending love back to them and letting them know you'll be connecting again.

Next, we'll connect with the Earth elements of the garden, which includes the soil and the rocks as well as any crystals you might have in the garden.

They all have consciousness, as do all beings on the Earth. First, we'll say hello to the microbial colonies that live in the soil; in healthy soil there can be 10 million of these bacteria per gram! Microbials are responsible for making the nutrients in the soil available to the plants, and their work is essential for a healthy garden.

Next, we have the rocks and the crystals, which carry their own unique frequencies and are very connected to us. We've used crystals as a way of healing and balancing for thousands of years on this planet. An example of this is when we use an amethyst crystal to promote spiritual awareness, inner peace, and positive transformation. Rocks have been used to enhance our life in the physical world for a very long time. We have used them for shelter, heat, tools, and much more. Our physical comfort would certainly not be the same without the help of the rock world.

To connect with the Earth elements, put your hand on your heart and send this world your love. Visualize the soil teeming with busy little microbes as they break down the nutrients to feed the plants. Say hello to the nutrients themselves and feel their vitality. Feel the energy of the rocks and the crystals, and say thank you to them for their service to humanity. Sit quietly and see whether you get a response; whatever you hear, see, or feel is perfect. This Earth-element world has so much love for us, as it's the foundation of our very selves. When we stop, connect with them, and say hello, their response is a joyous one. Ask whether they have a special message to give you, whether it's from the soil microbes, the rocks, or the crystals. Take it to heart and say thank you. Let them know you'll be connecting with them again, and send them love one more time as you say good-bye.

Next, we'll connect with the unseen realms of the Earth and your garden. Although these realms are not seen with our regular vision (except by folks who have either retained the sight from childhood or developed the ability in adulthood), they are very real. Life would not exist without them. These realms include the devas, nature spirits, faeries, gnomes, and other important nature beings. I'll explain who they are first, and then we'll have the opportunity to say hello to them in the garden.

Within the nature realms, the devas hold the archetypal pattern and plan for creation and wield its energy, while the elementals—the nature spirits—are the craftsmen who transform that energy into material form. The devas create the blueprints for all form; everything that is on this Earth (all form) was first thought of by the devas. They determine the shape, size, color, weight, life cycle, taste, and texture of everything that exists here. Everything in form has its own deva, and that deva has its own "computer file" of information pertinent to that particular form. We have, for instance, the Deva of Soil, the Deva of Shovels, the Deva of Computer Chips, *and* the Deva of Fuel Injection for your car! If it's here on the planet, the blueprint was created by a deva on the elemental level in tandem with human consciousness that desired to bring its invention into solid form. Although very few people even know the devas exist, that doesn't lessen their role in our lives, as everything on the Earth—all form—began as a thought in the elemental realms of the devas.

Next, we have the Nature Spirits. They take the devic blueprints and gather the earthly elements together to bring the design into actual form. For instance, after the Deva of carrots creates a carrot blueprint, a Nature Spirit will take a "drawing" of the seed and bring it into form on the Earth. The Nature Spirit will be connected to the core of that seed as it sprouts and grows and will bring that design to its completion.

Two other nature beings I'd like to introduce you to are the faeries and the gnomes. There are others you can connect with as well, such as the elves, the brownies, and "the little people," but I'll leave you to explore these wonderful beings on your own.

The Faerie Realm tends the energy of the plants, particularly the flowers. In their tending, they play among them. Faeries are winged beings, and they live in communities and family units similar to our own. The Faerie Realm colors the world with magic, and they bring light and joy to everything they touch.

The Gnomes are connected directly to the Earth. They work with the soil, the rocks, and the crystals, and their presence brings vitality to the Earth. They tend the Earth through the soil and through the roots of plants, and they live within the Earth, not on its surface.

It's as easy to connect to these unseen realms as it is to connect to the "seen" realms in your garden. Let's start with the Devic Realm.

Close your eyes and put your hand on your heart, filling it with love. Ask to be connected to the Devic Realm, particularly to the "Overlighting Deva" of your garden. (There are Overlighting Devas that oversee and control larger blueprints of a particular form, such as your garden.) Send the Deva your love and sit quietly, waiting for a response. What do you hear, see, or feel from the Deva? Let the Deva know that you are ready and willing to create a beautiful friendship with its overlighting presence and that your plan is to create heaven on Earth right there in your garden. Most likely, the Deva will be quite pleased to enter into a new cocreative partnership with you. You'll find that in working with the Deva your questions and concerns about the garden can be addressed, and you'll be delighted with the results. To receive this guidance, just ask your questions and see what answers you get. Whether you see, hear, or feel something or just get a hunch that you need to take action in a certain way, you'll be receiving information right from the source, and it doesn't get any better than that! Say thank you to the Overlighting Deva as well as to the other devas connected to your garden. Send them your love, letting them know you'll be connecting again soon.

Next, open your connection to the Nature Spirit Realm of your garden. There's a being known as Pan who is like the CEO of the Nature Spirit world, and you can connect with him directly in order to access the Nature Spirit Realm. (Nature spirits don't have genders, but Pan's essence feels more masculine to me.) With your hand on your heart, send your love, say hello, and see what response you get. Let Pan know that you've begun a cocreative partnership with all the nature beings in your garden and that you'd love to have his input as well. Feel the response. I'm sure Pan will be quite pleased to assist you in the garden. Then ask any questions you might have before closing the session, letting him know you'll be connecting again soon.

Next, we'll move into the Faerie Realm. Fill your heart with love, beauty, and joy (all faerie qualities), and send it out to the faeries. They'll return the feeling a hundredfold, and your heart will overflow with the joy they send back to you. Take in the feeling for a moment, and then let them know how much you appreciate the beauty they create in the garden and that you look forward to creating more with them. Send them your love once more, and say good-bye, letting them know you'll be "flying" with them again soon.

Lastly, we'll connect with the Gnomes. Send your love and appreciation to these steadfast and dedicated beings, thanking them for all the love and care they give to the Earth. See whether they have a response for you. They are generally quiet beings, but you'll feel their appreciation, as they so love to be honored for their work. Let them know you'll be connecting with them in the future concerning any questions you might have about your garden soil. Say good-bye, sending them your love once more and reminding them that you'll be checking in on a regular basis. They are the masters of soil, and you'll benefit greatly from their expertise.

With that, your session is complete. You've created a beautiful tapestry of connection with everyone in the garden, and the connection will only deepen with time.

Say thank you as you close, sending love to the garden once more. Let everyone know that you'll be checking in regularly and that you look forward to cocreating an amazing garden with them.

So, how do you proceed in the future using these new garden connections you've made? To keep it simple, you'll start by sending love to the garden (no need to put your hand on your heart, as that was an exercise to create heart awareness). From there, you might want to address your Overlighting Garden Deva or a specific nature being to speak about any cares, concerns, or questions you might have about the garden. As an example, if you were wondering how to create the healthiest garden soil you could, you would contact the Gnomes or the Overlighting Soil Deva to receive their input on the project. If you want to simplify things *even more* in this communication process, you can connect to the garden and ask whether *all* appropriate garden members will come forward to assist you in whatever you need. This automatically sets up a "conference call" and takes the guesswork out of figuring out who will be best to call on for the task at hand. Because you've already made a personal connection with so many of the nature beings in your garden, such as the insects, plants, and animals as well as the nature spirits, devas, and faeries, they'll all want to participate in these conference calls, as their expertise is needed. All you have to do is ask!

I know that if you have questions, these new communication tools will be helpful for you and that you'll soon be on your way to developing a wonderful working relationship with your garden. Remember to trust the process and keep the love flowing. Nature will take care of the rest.

In the next section, we'll be exploring the nuts and bolts of gardening, such as planning and planting the garden, choosing soil amendments, planting for pollinators, and much more. You'll find that now that you can talk to your garden, you'll step forward with confidence because you'll be able to communicate and cocreate with the garden every step of the way.

The Earth is changing and evolving, and you'll find these changes reflected in your garden. Therefore, don't be discouraged if it isn't always a smooth ride, as transitions aren't usually smooth and easy. Continue to keep the love flowing and be open to any hunches you receive about doing things differently in the garden, such as practicing different planting methods than you have in the past. Often the changes you make will be in better alignment with how you and the garden have evolved; it's important to keep listening as you both continue to evolve. Remember that it's a process, and try not to stress too much if your garden isn't perfect. The Earth is in the midst of a huge planetary shift, and you and your garden are part of that shift. All your garden helpers are on board to assist you any way they can, so keep the communication lines open. All you have to do is ask, and they'll be right there, ready to help!

So, let's get started on garden basics. It's time to put on the gloves, grab the shovels, and get down and dirty in the garden.

Are you ready for some fun?

2.

Part II
Getting Down to Business:
The Nuts and Bolts of Gardening

5

❖ ❖ ❖

*We come from the
Earth.
We return to the
Earth.
And in between
we garden.*

Having a successful garden is one of the most satisfying and, at times, most challenging things we can do. We love our gardens, but the learning curve can be steep sometimes. We often have to reach out to lots of folks along the way on our quest to becoming better gardeners. We talk to neighbors and friends, the guy at the hardware store, the folks at the nursery, or the gal at the farmers' market. We read books and magazines and maybe take a class or two. We find that gardens aren't just about connecting to nature. They're about connecting to people too! We share advice and food and make lifelong friends along the way. That's what makes the gardening world so special.

So, let's delve into that world a little more. We have so much to share as we expand on all things gardening.

In this part of the book, we'll cover the basics of gardening—the nuts and bolts, as I like to call it. Since it all begins with the soil, that's where we'll start. We'll expand from there. We'll cover compost and compost tea, soil tests and pH balance, organic amendments and NPK, soil structure and double digging, mulching and cover crops, and a whole lot more.

Next, we'll move into creating the garden plan, which explains what we want to plant and how we plan on doing it as well as tips on basic garden maintenance. We'll talk about choosing seeds and plants for your garden, planting in six-pack containers, direct sowing into the soil, rotating crops, planting for pollinators, using weather protection where needed, and setting up a basic maintenance plan to keep the garden healthy and vibrant all season long.

After that, we'll move into one of my favorite topics—harvesting and processing the "fruits" of our labor. It's really fun and rewarding to eat your garden bounty after seasons end, so we'll talk about freezing, drying, canning, and storing all that food you've grown.

When you have a pantry full of fresh food—your food—it's a beautiful thing. I love it, and I know you'll love it too!

Last but not least, we'll complete part 2 with an overview of the gardening cycles. This will include the equinox and solstice cycles as well as the cycle of completion, in which you put the garden to bed. We'll also talk about moon cycles and how our gardening activity can work with these cycles. It's really wonderful to observe the patterns of nature and to work within these patterns as we create and maintain our gardens. We find that our gardens are more balanced because we allow them to unfold within Nature's timing. And as we garden this way, we find ourselves more connected to Nature's timing as well. It's a good thing for everybody.

A healthy garden is part of a healthy planet, and it's well worth the effort. We're all in this together, so let's do the best we can to create a joy-filled and balanced world. Having an organic, cocreative garden is a very good place to start.

One

"Dishing the Dirt": It All Begins with the Soil

To forget how to
dig the Earth
and to tend the soil
is to forget ourselves.

—Mahatma Gandhi

As I hike in the mountains above the valley where I live, I find myself drawn to the beautiful, rich soil along the creeks and in the meadows as well as to the fluffy pine duff that lies at the base of trees in the forest. Those trees have dropped their needles for centuries, creating a beautiful mulch that nourishes them and the plants that grow beneath them. And every fall, all the mountain plants die back, adding to the mulch as they're covered with winter snow. This is the natural way of things, and it's what we want to create in our own gardens. So, how do we get there, you ask? Well, it's easy; we start with making our own compost. That's the best way to enrich the soil, just the way nature does it in the mountains. I do understand that some of you reading this don't have the time or energy to make compost. That's not a problem; there's ready-made compost at most nurseries or local garden centers. Just make sure you get the real deal. When it comes to buying compost, you get what you pay for. There are many good companies to choose from. I use products from Dr. Earth, EB Stone, and Whitney Farms, but there are lots of others. I personally don't use the low-end products that come from "sewage sludge," although some good companies do use it; again, you get what you pay for. If the product is inexpensive, it generally is less than ideal for super-healthy soil. The products that use quality ingredients cost more, but they're worth it. All those enriching ingredients are the key to developing rich, healthy soil in your garden, just as the rich soil in the mountains is created by a diversity of ingredients.

Now, for those folks who are into the whole compost thing, I have lots to share on the subject. First of all, what is compost? How is it defined? Put simply, compost is the digestion of plant matter. Digestion means to break into manageable parts. It's the same as when you eat a salad; you chew the vegetables so that they can be swallowed and assimilated as they go through your digestive tract. In composting, the plant matter is broken down into smaller particles, which then can be used to nourish the garden plants. As I said, the bigger the variety of ingredients that you use to make your compost, the better the nutrition available for your plants. Variety is, indeed, the spice of life, and that goes for the garden as well.

There are many ways to make compost, but most of them take a long time before you get your finished product. The method that I'll share with you is much quicker from start to finish; it's generally no longer than four weeks before you have beautiful compost. With that said, if you are interested in checking out composting methods other than what I offer here, you can browse the web or check out books specifically on composting. There's so much out there, and all methods work. It just depends on what your needs are. There are a few important things to consider when choosing your composting method. First, how much space do you have available? Then, what resources do you need to build or buy your composter? What materials do you have access to—that is, manure, grass clippings, and so on—to use in your compost? And last but very important, how much time and energy do you have for this composting project? All these things will help you decide which method is best for you. Our method works for us because we can make more compost in a short amount of time. We have a good-sized garden (about a thousand square feet of vegetable gardens as well as ten fruit trees, two rose gardens, and a variety of perennial flower/herb beds), so we need all the compost we can get. If you are starting a garden from scratch, even if it's a small one, it's nice to have the compost available in less time so you can dig it in and start planting sooner. This is especially true if you are starting out with poor soil. The more compost you have available, the richer your soil will become.

So, now here's the Vaughn Gardens method of composting. My husband, Steve, is actually the compost man. He does a great job, and I am grateful for his hard work and dedication. Way to go, Steve! The compost bins he uses are about the size of a trash can and are made with a piece of hardware cloth that he bends to make a circle. He then uses wires to tie the ends together. Steve says you can make it bigger or smaller, but the trash-can size seems about perfect. If you make it smaller, it's hard to get the shovel in to turn the ingredients. If you make it bigger, it takes longer to fill and "cook." He takes a piece of fabric—the stronger, the better—and encloses the outer surface of the bin with it, fastening it with staples, clothespins, or any similar method.

The fabric keeps the moisture in the compost at an even level, and it heats it up quicker as well. You can use a trash bag instead of fabric to enclose the bin, but it will break down in the sun fairly quickly. Steve is able to use the fabric covers for years before they succumb to the elements. That's definitely a good thing!

Now it's time to fill the compost bin. Steve uses a variety of "ingredients" to create the beautiful compost that nourishes our garden. The first rule is to create a balance between green and brown materials. Green materials are fresh, wet vegetable matter, whereas brown materials are dry, weathered matter. For instance, grass clippings are green materials, and we keep them and use them throughout the growing season. We also save most of the trimmings from the flower beds; we cut them up in small pieces so they'll break down easier. Being full of nitrogen, they're also a green material. We gather fallen leaves in autumn and store them in trash bags; they provide the brown materials needed to balance the green in the compost pile. If you have the opportunity to gather some of these materials before you start your compost bin, you'll have a head start on the whole process. If you don't have a lawn, you can always gather clippings from other folks. Just make sure they're organic. You don't want grass grown with chemicals in your compost pile. And if you don't have enough leaves to gather in your yard, I'm sure your neighbors will be more than happy to share some of theirs, especially if you offer to rake them up!

We also have access to animal manures. We use horse and llama poop. They're a great nitrogen activator, which means they heat up the pile through a chain of microbial activity. Manure is a great soil amendment in and of itself, because it replenishes the soil with essential elements while also adding humus. When we add it to the compost pile, all its benefits become part of the compost, which makes the compost even better. The only thing you have to watch out for with animal manures are the potassium levels. Potassium is an essential part of plant processes, but too much is not desirable. This is when doing a commercial soil test comes in handy. We do a test once a year, and if we find that our potassium levels are above average, we use gypsum to remedy the problem. Gypsum is derived from the naturally occurring mineral calcium sulfate, and it lessens or relieves high-potassium soils. It has been helpful to us when we've needed it. I'll expand on the value of soil tests a little later in the book.

So, getting back to the compost bin, once you've filled it with a mix of brown and green ingredients, use your shovel and mix it all together, making sure to mix in the stuff on the bottom as well. Steve made a special long-handled shovel for this job (he calls it the "back-saver shovel"), but any shovel will do. Once you've mixed all the ingredients together, wet it down, making sure to get the edges of the bin wet as well. The compost needs to be the consistency of a moist sponge. Steve keeps a cover over it—a piece of fabric is perfect—which helps to keep the top from drying out, especially during the summer heat. If you are continuing to add ingredients, just mix them in each day until the bin is full, about four to six inches from the top, watering the bin as needed to keep it moist. From there, you let it sit and do its thing. How do you know it's doing its thing, you ask? Well, that's when you break out your handy-dandy compost thermometer. A compost thermometer looks like a meat thermometer only a whole lot bigger. You can find one at most garden centers or in gardening catalogs. You use it to keep track of what the compost is doing and to know when the cycle is done. You stick it in the center of the pile and let it sit for a few minutes, and it will register the temperature within a minute or two. You might want to write the temperatures down in a journal so you can record how many days it took for your pile to heat up (to 160°F or so) as well as how many days it took to cool down again (usually to 50–55°F or so). With this information, you'll be able to gauge how long it will take you to get your finished product. Steve has a garden journal to record the compost temperatures as well as other events in the garden. It has been helpful for him to keep records from each gardening season, so he can build on what worked in the past. He has found, however, that with a changing climate, it's been important for him to adapt to new ways of doing things in the garden and not depend so much on the records. He still uses them, but he stays open if things need to be done differently.

Anyway, back to compost. When the bin reaches its max of about 160°F, that usually lasts five to seven days before it starts cooling down. It heats up much quicker in the summer than in the winter, so you'll have more finished product to work with during the summer, especially in climates with a well-defined seasonal pattern. Once the pile cools down to about 60–70°F, it's finished and available to put out in the garden. You might get a little blue mold in your pile from time to time. If so, don't worry. You can eliminate it with extra mixing; aeration always does the trick. It's important to keep your compost aerated on a regular basis, as this assists in the breakdown process and alleviates strong odors.

Here's a quick review for making good compost:

1. Brown materials—Dry, weathered material. They are complex carbon compounds for energy. The microbial oxidation of the carbon compounds produces the heat for the pile. They need to comprise 50 percent of the pile's ingredients.
2. Green materials—Fresh, wet, green vegetable matter. This provides nitrogen basics, growing and reproducing more organisms to oxidize the plant material. They comprise the other half (50 percent) of the pile's ingredients.
3. Oxygen—Mixing the pile is needed for aerobic digestion of the carbon compounds in the decomposition process. (Otherwise, it gets stinky!)
4. Water—In the right amounts, it maintains the digestive activity in the compost. The consistency of the pile needs to be that of a dried-out sponge. (Too much water can cause anaerobic conditions, which can also make the pile smell like rotten eggs!)

So, now we're on to the kitchen scraps part of the composting process. There are various methods that people use to break down their kitchen waste. I will share the method that I use. Again, check books or the Internet for ideas if you're curious about other ways to do it. I have a compost crock in the kitchen that I use to collect my scraps. Any container will do as long as it has a lid to keep out the flies. If ants are a problem, you can keep it in the fridge. Don't put any meat or dairy in the compost—veggies, fruits, coffee grounds, egg shells, and so on are perfect. If you want your scraps to break down quicker, cut them up in small pieces before you put them in the crock. Once it's full, I put it outside in a big plastic box with a lid on it. (A small trash can would work as well.) If critters such as bears, raccoons, or skunks are a problem in your area, you'll have to come up with something more heavy duty, or keep the container inside, away from nighttime foragers. I keep emptying the crock into the box until it's full (and stinky, I might add!), and then I pour the gloppy mess into a compost tumbler. There are many compost tumblers on the market, but they all consist of a drum on a stand that spins or tumbles the compost. This aerates the kitchen scraps so they can break down. When I add the scraps, I add to the mix about a five-gallon bucket's worth of brown leaves along with a product called compost activator, and I tumble it every day. (Compost activators can be found in most nurseries and garden catalogs).

As with Steve's compost bin, once it's full, I don't add any more ingredients. I just tumble it every day until it's ready to go. Using a compost tumbler for kitchen scraps instead of putting them in open bins means that you don't attract animals to the compost. That's why I do the scraps separately from the bin. It works out really well. I don't use the compost thermometer for the compost tumbler. Once the food has broken down (meaning that it is no longer a stinky, gloppy mess—it's more dry and uniform in appearance), it's time to empty it onto a tarp and give it to Steve. The compost will finish its breaking-down process in his bin. By that time, the food is no longer attractive to animals, and it completes the composting process quickly.

Another method worth noting for breaking down kitchen scraps is earthworm composting. This is an especially fun project for kids. There are special earthworm boxes you can buy, or you can make your own. An earthworm box needs to stay moist and dark but never soggy, and there needs to be a cover to keep light out of the box. You feed the worms fresh scraps each day, and it's important to chop the scraps in the blender first. The earthworms have difficulty ingesting anything much larger than the size of their mouths, so chopping is important. The best worms for worm composting (also known as vermicomposting) are red worms, or red wigglers. They are a different species from common garden worms and night crawlers, both of which need large amounts of soil and cool temperatures to survive. One pound of red worms (about a thousand worms) is enough to start a worm bin. You can buy them from a worm farm or bait shop, and once your bin is established, you'll have enough to share with others who might be interested in vermicomposting. A medium-sized worm box can process more than five pounds of food waste each week. They quickly turn your kitchen scraps into an exceptionally rich fertilizer (known as worm castings) that is ideal for your garden and your houseplants. There's lots of information on the Internet about vermicomposting, including how to set up your box, what kind of boxes are available, and even how to build your own. There's also a fun book you can check out called *Worms Eat My Garbage*, by May Appelhof. Vermicomposting is a fun thing to try, especially if kids are involved. It's another fun way to turn your garbage into gold!

Once my compost is ready to go, I have a special "garden drink" I make with it. It's called compost tea. All you need is a five-gallon bucket full of water and a burlap sack. You put the finished compost in the burlap sack, close it at the top, and put it in the bucket of water. Let it steep for a few weeks until it gets nice and "fragrant." (*Stinky* is the word!) Then pull the burlap bag out and use the liquid as a soil drench for all your garden plants, pouring the tea directly at the root zone. The tea-brewing process extracts nutrients and, in some cases, multiplies beneficial bacteria and fungi from the compost. It suspends nutrients in the water in a form that makes them quickly available to the plants. I always think of compost tea as a natural super charge for the garden. It's especially good for new plantings and plants that are struggling. It's a wonderful addition to your regular garden maintenance, easy to make and easy to use. A wonderful thing, indeed!

That wraps up the chapter on composting. Once you've got your fresh compost made, you can dig it into your annual vegetable beds, use it throughout the growing season as a top dressing, or do both. In this way, it will provide mulch and nutrients as it gets watered into the soil. Fresh compost is the ultimate recyclable material, and it provides a huge boost to the garden. That's why I'm so enthusiastic about singing its praises as one of the best things you can do for the garden! So get out there and have fun making all that black gold. And when your garden starts shining, you'll be happy you did.

Two

THE SCOOP ON SOIL TESTS

$\mathcal{L}$et's face it, folks; there are very few, if any, of us that have the good fortune of starting a garden with great soil. It seems like there's always something that needs to be balanced, and that's when taking a soil test comes in handy. It takes the guesswork out of what you might need to amend your soil. In this chapter, I'll give you a basic outline of what is measured with a soil test and how those measurements relate to the health or deficiencies of your garden soil. With that understanding, you'll be able to decide whether you want to get one for your garden or not.

Soil pH. First, we'll discuss the pH factor. The term *pH* describes the alkalinity (sweetness) or acidity (sourness) of soil, compost, or some other substance. The pH is usually expressed as a number. The pH scale runs from 1, indicating pure acidity, to 14, indicating pure alkalinity. Something neutral would be described as 7, halfway between 1 and 14. The neutral zone (approximately 7) is desirable for a wide range of plants, so that's a good range for your garden soil. To break it down further, most flowers and vegetables enjoy a slightly acidic soil (6.0 to 6.8), whereas true acid-loving plants, such as berries, potatoes, and azaleas, do better with a pH of 5. There are other plants, such as beets, lilacs, and some lilies, that actually tend to do better in slightly alkaline soils, above 7.

So, with that said, what do you use to balance your soil pH? If your soil is too acidic, there are things you can use to "sweeten" it. These will raise the pH, making it more alkaline. Lime or crushed limestone, ground clam shells, crushed oyster shells, wood ashes, dolomite, and bone meal are good sweeteners. If your soil is too alkaline, there are products available to make your soil more sour. They are gypsum—calcium sulfate—and elemental sulfur. If you decide to get a soil test, you'll see where your pH balance lies, and you can amend your soil accordingly. The important thing to remember is that soil pH is the key to the release of essential nutrients to plants. If the level is not appropriate for the plants you are growing, they won't be able to absorb what they need from the soil.

Organic Matter. This is what is known as humus. Good soil should have enough decayed plant and other organic matter (anywhere from 3.5 percent to 8 percent by volume) to increase air penetration into the soil by making it more "fluffy" and to improve drainage in claylike soils. It is also used to improve water retention in sandy soils and to loosen the soil for better root penetration so that soil microbes can flourish. Humus should penetrate as much as eight to twenty inches below your garden soil's surface. This is where the beauty of compost really shines. All the organic matter that you cooked in your compost provides a high humus content for your garden soil. It's important to dig the compost into the double length of a shovel (eighteen to twenty-four inches) so that it can really do its job of creating a fluffy layer of humus in the soil. Creating rich, fluffy soil through the incorporation of organic matter is one of the keys to a healthy garden. A soil test will give you a percentage number for the amount of organic matter found in your soil. Based on that percentage, you can amend your soil accordingly.

NPK. This stands for nitrogen, phosphorus, and potassium, respectively.

1. Nitrogen is one of the primary nutrient requirements for all life. It is found in every living cell as a part of protein. Small amounts of nitrogen are added to the soil through rainfall. Nitrogen is released as nitrates by the continuing decay of organic material in soil. Some organic amendments high in nitrogen are blood meal, bat guano, alfalfa meal, and fish meal. There are also liquid fertilizers (such as fish emulsion and kelp) that contain plenty of nitrogen to give a quick boost to your plants.
2. Phosphorus is the key element that plants need for flowering, fruiting, and rooting. You find it organically in products such as bone meal or rock phosphate (which is actually ancient bone piles). It is

normally found in nature combined with calcium in the form of calcium phosphate. In this form, the phosphorus tends to remain locked up with calcium, which means it is not available to plants as it is. It must be unlocked in the soil through natural microbial and chemical processes. It is crucial, then, to have phosphorus in adequate quantity as well as to have healthy, balanced, bioactive soil to make it available to the plants.

3. Potassium (potash) exists in most types of organic matter. It is critical for plant vigor, as it is the basis of many plant functions, causing plants to manufacture sugars, proteins, and amino acids. (Plants need them just as we do.) It also aids in the formation of flowers. Potassium strengthens plant tissue and makes vegetation more disease resistant. Plants that receive too little potash look stunted. Some folks use wood ash as a potassium amendment, although you don't always know how much potash is in the ash. A better source is green sand. This is mined from a natural organic deposit of shells and organic matter deposited on ancient sea floors millions of years ago. Green sand releases potash into the soil slowly, mimicking the natural tendency of the soil to gradually make potassium available. There have been times when I have taken soil tests on my garden and found that the potassium levels were too high, probably due to the high potassium-content use. When this has occurred, we remedied the imbalance by using gypsum, which lessened the potassium levels in our soil.

4. Calcium is a very abundant element in nature. It is an important element that plants and humans require for cell growth. Since plants are made of millions of cells, and calcium is a critical element in the structure of cell walls, you can see how important this element is. Seldom is it lacking, but there are times when it can actually be too high. In this case, you end up with an alkaline condition (high pH), which can impede plant absorption of some nutrients. This is when you add soil sulfur to remedy the high pH (for the type of plants you are growing) and bring the soil back into balance.

Magnesium is a component of chlorophyll, and, like potassium, it is important for plant metabolic processes and the uptake of phosphorus. It is naturally found in some types of clay soils. In fact, there's an old-timer story that says you can tell how much magnesium there is in your soil by the thickness of the dirt that sticks to your boots. If your soil is lacking in magnesium, you can apply rock phosphates, dolomite lime, or Epsom salts to remedy the problem.

If you have too much magnesium, this can bind up your soil so that water and nutrients don't penetrate well. Too much magnesium can also cause a high pH. In this case, gypsum can be added to leach out the excess.

Sulfur is used by plants in the manufacture of amino acids and the production of proteins and vitamins, particularly B1 and biotin.

Zinc aids vegetables and fruits in developing their sweet taste.

Manganese helps the enzyme system of plants and aids in chlorophyll formation and photosynthesis.

Iron acts as a coenzyme in oxidation and other metabolic processes.

Copper helps disease resistance and makes strong stalks.

Boron controls the quality and taste of food crops and helps with disease resistance.

There are two more important aspects that will be analyzed in your soil test. The first is called CEC, which stands for the cation exchange capacity of the soil. This reveals your soil's nutrient capacity. The second is called cation saturation, which indicates the percent of your soil's total plant food–holding capacity that is actually taken up by positively charged ions of certain soil elements. The CEC is any soil's capacity to hold positively charged plant nutrients. The charge is what makes it possible for nutrients to pass into root systems. Typically, cations such as Potassium (K+), Magnesium (Mg+), Calcium (CA+), and Hydrogen (H+) are determined by the soil's amount and kind of clay and humus. The larger the value, the more positive cations the soil can hold. This measures the plant food–holding capacity of the soil. When you receive the results of a soil test, these figures will be part of your analysis, and you'll be given recommendations on how to remedy any imbalance that might be present.

If you choose to also test for micronutrients, your test will include numbers for zinc, manganese, iron, copper, and boron. These elements are critical for plant metabolic functions, but they're not needed in very large quantities. A trace element will only help a soil from which the element is missing, and excessive levels can actually impede the plant's ability to take up other nutrients; be careful when you use them as amendments—keep a light touch for sure. With that said, even though minute quantities are used, the absence of any of these crucial elements can have devastating effects on your crops, so it is a good idea to include them in your soil test. Amendments of these elements come from various mining processes and are frequently sulfated to make the plant's nutrients available.

So, that's the scoop on soil testing. Early spring is the perfect time to take a soil test for your garden. You can check for lab services through your state university extension service. Also, an organic gardening company called Peaceful Valley has a soil-test service available through their catalog. You can always browse the Internet to see all the options available for soil tests and go from there. All soil tests include instructions on how to take the test, and those that you mail in will include a preaddressed, postage-paid package for mailing to the lab as part of the order. Taking a yearly soil test takes the guesswork out of garden-soil maintenance. I'd compare it to taking a blood test to see how our bodies are doing and what nutrients we might be lacking. It's the same thing with the garden. And it sets the stage, so to speak, for a successful and bountiful gardening season.

Three

SOIL AMENDMENTS 101

In almost every garden,
the land is made better
and so is the gardener.

—Robert Rodale

Here are many organic soil amendments on the market as well as several good specialty mixes for roses and other flowers, vegetables, fruit trees, acid-loving plants, all-purpose balanced blends, and so on. These organic blends take the guesswork out of what we might need to feed our roses, for example, and they're effective and easy to use. I encourage you to check out the various blends at your local nursery and try a few to see what works for you. Meanwhile, I'll provide a quick rundown of the amendments you might find in these blends. They are also good just used on their own, if there's something particular that is needed in your garden.

Here's the amendment list:

Blood meal is an organic source of readily available nitrogen. It can be added to compost to speed decomposition. It is an excellent source for a slow release of nitrogen. (It is one of the highest nonsynthetic sources of nitrogen at 13.25 percent nitrogen.)

Bone meal provides a gentle, long-lasting source of phosphorus and nitrogen. It can assist in balancing acidic soils.

Green sand is mixed from a natural oceanic deposit of shells and organic matter deposited on ancient sea floors millions of years ago. It is an important source of potassium, releasing the potash to the soil slowly. It is best to apply this to the soil before planting.

Alfalfa meal is a rich source of natural organic ingredients. It provides a gentle source of nutrients for your garden. Its excellent carbon-to-nitrogen ratio will facilitate quick decay in the soil. It is especially good on roses, in vegetable gardens, and in the compost pile.

Bat guano is an excellent source of nutrients, especially nitrogen, for your garden. Use it to make bat-guano tea, which is great for transplants and plants that are stressed. Mix one tablespoon in a gallon of water. Let it sit overnight. When watering plants, add one cup of tea to every gallon of water used.

Cottonseed meal is an excellent source of natural, slow-release nutrients, therefore it is nonburning and safe to use on young plants. It is an acidic-based fertilizer and is especially useful for acidifying alkaline soils and feeding acid-loving plants.

Rock phosphate is the mined remains of ancient marine life and prehistoric animals. Naturally rich in phosphorus, it is released slowly into the soil through the actions of soil microorganisms. It is important for root development, is a major factor in determining the growth and vigor of a plant, and has a role in flower, fruit, and seed production.

Kelp meal is a great general-purpose soil conditioner. It contains natural growth hormones and is a great source of trace elements.

Feather meal is a byproduct of processing poultry. Containing up to 12 percent nitrogen, it is a source of slow-release, organic, high-nitrogen fertilizer. It increases green-leaf growth, activates compost decomposition, and improves soil structure.

Sulfur (elemental sulfur) is useful for balancing pH when the soil is too alkaline. (It sours the soil.) It is used by plants in the manufacture of amino acids and the production of proteins and vitamins, particularly B1 and biotin.

Dolomite lime is derived from a naturally occurring limestone deposit. It is intended to help correct the pH of acid soils by sweetening the soil. It also provides a natural source of calcium and magnesium, both of which are important plant nutrients.

Gypsum is derived from the naturally occurring mineral calcium sulfate. It is the source of two valuable plant nutrients, calcium and sulfur, in a readily available and soluble form. It can help to loosen heavy clay soils, promoting better root growth as well as more efficient water and fertilizer use.

Chicken manure is good to use at the time when you are preparing your garden beds. It is a great source of nitrogen, although it can burn plants, so use it sparingly.

Ironite is a blend of ingredients that provides nitrogen and vital trace elements—calcium, magnesium, sulfur, cobalt, iron, manganese, molybdenum, and zinc.

Epsom salts are a great source of magnesium. They are good for roses if magnesium is needed.

There's also a variety of liquid amendments to choose from. They're in concentrated form, so you have to dilute them first before application. They can be used as a soil drench by pouring them at the base of trees or plants. Or use them as a foliar spray by spraying the leaves of plants or trees with the diluted liquid. A foliar spray is best to use when the temperature is eighty degrees or below because the leaves' stomata (where the fertilizer is absorbed under the leaves) naturally close during hot temperatures, so the spray won't be absorbed as efficiently. My favorite is a blend of fish emulsion and kelp. The fish emulsion is a good source of fast-acting nitrogen. The kelp, which also has a fair amount of nitrogen, contains trace elements and natural growth hormones as well. (Look at how quickly kelp grows in the ocean!)

There are many sprayers to choose from for applying the liquid amendments. They're all good, whether you choose a hose-end sprayer, a small handheld sprayer, or a bigger three-gallon tank. It just depends on what your needs are. I have a handheld sprayer, and I use a gallon jug to dilute the organic concentrate. Then I pour the dilution into the sprayer. That way I don't have to drag a big tank around the yard like I used to do. Some folks have a harness that they use to carry a tank around on their backs, which probably works great. Again, it all depends on what works best for you.

Organic liquid fertilizers provide a quick boost of nutrients and microbial activity directly to the plants. They are especially effective used during the spring because of all the new growth that occurs at that time. There are many wonderful organic liquid fertilizers available, so check at your local nursery or garden center or on garden websites.

I'm going to close this soil chapter with a beautiful message from the Nature Spirits of my garden:

You say that soil is everything, and we couldn't agree more. But you've left out the most important ingredient in this discussion, and that ingredient is love. It's every bit as important as all the other ingredients you listed that are good for the soil. Yes, you must put love into the soil as you work and play in the garden. With each strike of your shovel, each amendment you use, each soil test you take, each liquid you measure and pour onto the soil, there must be love in it. The love needs to flow from your heart, through your eyes, down your arms, and into the garden. We feel your love; we taste it, touch it, and relish in it. When it pours from your heart, it enlivens the soil every bit as much as the amendments do. So, let it flow through your shovels, your rakes, your wheelbarrows—all your tools—and we will smile back with dazzling flowers, tasty vegetables, and luscious fruits. Remember, it's all about the love.

Four

Let's Plant a Garden

The best place to seek God
is in the garden.
You can dig for him there.

—George Bernard Shaw

Ask any gardener for the story of their first diggings in the dirt, and I'm sure they'll weave a wonderful tale of joy for you. That's because gardening is, after all, pure joy, and most gardeners remember the first time they felt it.

My gardening joy began when I was maybe eight years old or so. There were four kids in the family at the time (little sis came along later), and my mom bought each of us a packet of seeds. We had our own little plots on the south side of the house—I remember them well—and she helped us plant our little gardens. My older brother, Bobby, planted lettuce. My older sister, Bev, planted pansies. My younger brother, Kenny, planted radishes. And I planted zinnias. Bobby's and Bev's plots struggled with the south Florida heat, while Kenny's radishes thrived in the sun. Meanwhile, my happy little zinnias grew strong and tall, and it was just a matter of time before my little plot looked like a rainbow. The gardening bug got me good way back when, and I've loved to play in the garden—particularly in the flowers—ever since! I say thank you to my mom for igniting that gardening spark in me and, of course, to that little packet of zinnia seeds that started it all.

With this next section of the book, we'll be talking about planning and planting the garden. Where you live will dictate when planting time begins. The tropics generally have their best growing season through the winter, whereas places such as the low desert grow best from late winter into spring. Other areas, including mine in the high desert of California, usually plant anywhere from April through June, depending on their latitude (and possibly altitude). Of course, if you live in the southern hemisphere, then planting begins in many areas around November or December.

Often, folks start browsing garden-seed catalogs during their gardening rest time. That's when we let go of last year's garden and start dreaming of the new one to come. There's some great organic seed companies out there—more than ever, I'm happy to report—and this is the time to check out what's available and decide what you'd like to grow for the coming year. Whether you shop online, in garden catalogs, at nurseries, or even at big department stores, there are wonderful varieties of organic seeds available at most places, giving you many options to choose from.

Now, there are some of you folks who aren't interested in starting your garden from seed. I understand how you feel, as it's a bigger time commitment to nurture plants from seed to sprout to being mature enough for planting. In that case, when the actual planting season begins in your area, the nurseries and garden centers will be stocked with lots of plants to choose from. It isn't always easy, however, to find plants that have been grown organically, although availability is getting better as more consumers choose to grow organic. In some areas, such as rural areas with smaller populations, the pickings for organic plants can be slim. In that case, you have to grow your vegetables and flowers from seed in order to grow organically. If you are growing from seed, there are options on how you want to do your planting. Do you want to start them indoors and then plant them in the garden when the weather warms up? Or, do you want to direct sow them into the garden soil at the proper planting time for your area? Or do you want to do a little bit of both?

If you want to plant them in containers first, you'll need to gather a few materials together for that process. Either visiting a nursery or browsing a garden catalog will give you lots of ideas on how you want to start your seeds. There are seed trays with little planting cubicles that look like ice-cube trays, only bigger. They allow you to start many seeds in one planter. You can also recycle plastic six-pack planting containers. Most nurseries have them in their recycling section and will give them to you for free. Another option is to start your plants in individual pots. You can use plastic pots or even peat pots. The peat pots decompose, so you plant them directly into the garden, which is a cool thing. Next, you'll need to buy your organic seed-starting mix, which is made specifically for good seed germination. Most blends contain a mix of Canadian *Sphagnum*, peat moss, and either perlite or vermiculite (which keeps the mix from packing down). A good seed-starting mix ensures the best germination for your seeds, even the tiniest ones! Once your seeds are planted, you have to decide where you want them to grow. Most folks set them up somewhere in the house—a sunny windowsill is perfect. Most seeds need warm soil to germinate—65–70°F is ideal—so it's best to place them inside unless you have a heated greenhouse. There's a great gardeners' aid for optimal seed germination called a germination mat. It's a heating pad for seeds! You place your seed trays or pots on the mat and plug it in. It keeps them at the perfect temperature (not too hot) for quick germination. Once the seeds have germinated, it keeps the plant roots warm so they grow quickly. Most seed trays come with a clean plastic lid that fits over the top. This provides a moist environment for the seedlings to grow.

I start my seeds in six-pack planting containers, so I make little toothpick-and-plastic coverings for them. The toothpicks are the supports, and I lay the piece of clear plastic wrap over them. This forms a mini greenhouse over the plants, which helps them to germinate. Once they're about two inches tall, I remove the plastic and toothpicks and save them for next year. It's always best to ensure good germination by planting a few seeds in each pot, but don't overdo it! (My husband used to be famous for that—he finally learned.) For most vegetables, such as tomatoes, peppers, and so on, I'll put two seeds in each planting hole. For herbs such as basil and dill, I'll put in about a half-dozen seeds.

I usually direct sow a lot of my seeds into the garden. If you live in a place with a defined winter season, then cool-weather crops such as peas, lettuce, kale, and beets can be planted in early spring. If you want the seeds to germinate quicker and grow better outdoors, you can cover them with hoop houses (also called grow tunnels). A hoop house consists of prebent PVC pipes or wire frames that are covered with a clear plastic sheet and staked down on all sides. You place them over the garden bed and plant your seeds inside. The hoop house provides extra warmth and weather protection for germination and for good plant growth. Of course, if you live in the tropics, cold protection is not an issue for you. When I lived in San Diego, I never knew about hoop houses, but when I moved to the high desert of California (with its late-spring frosts), I learned what a difference these season extenders can make in having healthier plants and an earlier harvest. On warm days, it's best to open the hoop house, providing the plants with direct sunshine and fresh air. They also need watering from time to time, as they're covered and unable to receive any moisture that falls. Eventually, when the weather warms up and they've out grown their cozy home, it's time to take the hoop house down. The plants are strong and able to grow without protection, so the hoops are put away for later use. We actually use them again in the fall. We plant lettuce and garlic, and keep the crops covered for the winter. They're developing their roots all winter long and really take off in the spring. We used to leave these plants uncovered, but we found they do so much better if they're covered for the cold. The protection seems to give them a head start so that they grow by leaps and bounds when the weather warms up in the spring.

One more invaluable season extender I will mention is something called walls o' water. (There's another kind, just as effective, called cozy coats.) They're a plastic sleeve that is placed around a plant at planting time. The walls o' water have eighteen tubes that are filled with water, making them freestanding (although you can use stakes to give them more support, especially in the wind). The water acts like insulation, storing heat during the day and releasing it slowly at night. All of the seedlings we start in the house are planted in these walls o' water in the garden in May. They keep the roots warm and protect the tender plants from the late-spring frosts that we get from time to time. We usually harden off our indoor plants in April, which means we get them used to being outdoors by placing them on the porch on sunny days and bringing them back inside at night. By the time May rolls around, they're accustomed to the sunshine and ready to be put in the ground (and placed in their walls o' water, of course).

There are some plants we direct sow into the garden in May, and we don't use walls o' water for them. They are fast growing, so they don't need to be planted earlier to give them time to grow, as is necessary with the peppers and tomatoes. These include squash, beans, cucumbers, and cilantro as well as flowers such as zinnias and cosmos. If a spring frost does come through, however, we'll protect them beforehand by covering them with a piece of frost cloth. This is lightweight fabric, sold specifically for this use, that keeps the plants about four degrees warmer, which is usually enough to protect them from getting nipped from the cold. You can find all these season extenders at the nursery or in garden catalogs. They are invaluable when you need to keep your plants protected from the elements.

When you begin to plant, keep in mind that most plants need some kind of support system. Tomato cages are great for tomatoes, peppers, tomatillos, eggplant, and basil. Squash and potatoes don't need support, but remember that they do need lots of room to grow. The same goes for melons and cucumbers, although you might need to set up a trellis for the cucumbers so the fruit can be suspended off the ground.

There are lots of ready-made support systems you can buy for your vegetable garden, or you can make your own. For our runner bean vines, Steve bought some old aluminum ladders and took them apart, using each ladder as a support for the vines. He dug each ladder into the ground about a foot deep and tied strings on them, giving the beans a chance to wind their way onto the ladders. I thought it was a pretty cool use for ladders he found in the junkyard!

A good rule of thumb for planting is to always give your plants more room than you think they'll need. What looks like so much space when you first do your planting can turn into a jungle at the height of gardening season. What Steve and I do, before we do any planting, is to map out our garden design on paper. We've already chosen the plants we want to grow for the season (and ordered any seeds we might need). We draw an outline for each garden bed. (We have several beds, but even if you have only one bed, a map is still helpful.) We discuss which plants will go in each bed and decide on their placement in the bed, and then we write their names in the space we've chosen for them. When it's time to plant the garden, we just follow the map(s) and plant accordingly. This helps with crop rotation. For those not familiar with crop rotation, the idea is to move various plant families (such as the nightshade family, which includes tomatoes) around instead of planting the same plants in the same spot every year. This practice has many benefits for your garden. First of all, it mitigates the buildup of pathogens and garden critters, which can become pests when they're out of balance. Crop rotation also improves soil structure and fertility, particularly if you alternate deep-rooted plants with those that are shallow rooted. For example, in one area, we'll grow onions the first year, tomatoes the next, kale and chard the next, and summer squash the year after that. Different plant families, different root systems. Even if you have a single garden bed, you can still move the types of plants you want to grow from one section of the bed to another. This is still practicing crop rotation, because the different plants (with their different root systems) will ensure a healthier garden as they're moved around the garden bed from year to year. Steve and I save the garden maps each year so we can reference them when creating a new garden plan. It's a lot easier to have it on paper than to try to depend on your memory from years past.

Even with the best of soil and good garden planning, it's still important to put a little extra organic fertilizer into the planting hole when digging in your annual vegetable plants and seeds. This will ensure that they'll get just what they need when they need it the most—when they're first starting out in the garden. As I mentioned in an earlier chapter, there are many good organic fertilizers to choose from. An all-purpose vegetable food would be great for seeds and seedlings. Just put a handful in the planting hole, mix it with soil, and carefully (with a blessing) place the seed or plant in the hole, backfilling it with soil. Water the plant or seed in well, and stick a plant label in the ground (if you have one). Send the plant or seed your love, welcoming it to its new home. It's so important to provide a good growing environment for your seedlings, as you have done. With all the efforts you've made, they will grow to their full potential.

The next chapter is all about creating a beautiful and balanced garden for the pollinators. A healthy ecosystem is one full of diversity, and this can start in your own backyard. When you plant with pollinators in mind, your garden becomes multifaceted. It provides food and beauty for you and wild forage for all the bees, butterflies, hummingbirds, and lots of other critters that will call your garden their home. Creating a garden plan is fun, and fun is what gardening is all about! So, let's see what we can do to make your garden a little slice of paradise for everyone.

Conversations with Steve's Tools
by Mary Tannheimer

Three regular-sized wheelbarrows and one kid-sized wheelbarrow full of compost are sleeping in the sun. I touch one.

Wheelbarrow: "Oh (waking up with the equivalent of stretching), you're here."
Mary: "Yes. Can you talk now?"
Wheelbarrow: "Of course."
Mary: "What is your experience like in the garden here?"
Wheelbarrows (all chuckling): "Oh, well, hmmmm...We like it. We keep each other company, and our companionship makes the loads lighter and the work easier. We sing work songs, and the days pass well."
Mary: "You're all in good repair, I see."
Wheelbarrows: "Yes. He [Steve] cares about us, so he makes sure we all operate well. This is important to us and our well-being. We operate in the domain of entropy (composting), and we don't want to go there [entropy] until it's our time. Good care is important to us, because we work hard. We need respect, too."

They show me a picture of a man ("Usually it is men. They're much more aggressive.") dumping a wheelbarrow, pushing it roughly away, and letting it crash to a halt and fall over.

Wheelbarrows: "*So* disrespectful! We don't need this! Push somebody else around if you need to! *Not* us!"
Mary: "OK, OK—got the picture!"
Wheelbarrows: "All your behaviors out here go right into the food. Think about it. You want to eat anger? No, right? Be gentle with us. We can work *really* hard, so the right treatment is in order here. A happy garden means a happy stomach!

"Keep us clean and oiled, tires full, handles tight. Give us a pat at the end of the day, and say, 'Good job, boys! Good job, girls!' You'll know who is who if you feel it out. Put us away with pride. We're proud of ourselves. We have a long and illustrious lineage throughout history. You couldn't have done it without us. Right, boys?"
Many more voices: "Yeah! For sure! Right!"

Group voice: "No more crash-and-burn landings, OK? We're proud and capable tools in the right hands. *Make sure* those hands are yours!"

Now it's on to the shovels. They feel proud and solitary, like spears across the warrior's shoulders. They are somewhat reserved, but they are friendly with each other.

Mary: "What is your experience in the garden?"
Shovels: "We gird ourselves for the day like soldiers, for our life is hard. Here we are treated with respect, but usually we are carelessly thrown about. Our purpose is a grave one—ha, a little humor here—often literally so."

I hear lots of chuckling and feel them slapping each other on the back.

Shovels: "Shovels do serious business in the world, accessing areas invisible to the common glance, requiring grit (ha ha), perseverance, and courage."

They show me a picture of a small group of strong, burly men with armbands of shining metal. They are wearing furs, like Vikings.

Shovels: "We are a small, specialized group, made for specialized work. We are *not* hammers! If you need a hammer, get one. We are sleek and sharp and strong, like sharks, ready to take a bite out of the ground. Yet if left to our own methods, we would bless the ground on our way down and slice cleanly in, sharp and quiet like a scalpel, lessening the pain of entry. We would sing healing songs to the Mother to atone for our creation of pain. Something to think about, eh? Digging would be easier this way for you, instead of *hammering* and *twisting* us around in the ground with aggression, letting out your pent-up frustrations. Smoother is better, actually. Smooth and clean. Concentration and precision, like a surgeon. We are *cutting* tools, and that's how we work the best. Keep us clean and sharp, like a well-driven mind, and we'll serve you for many years, with oiled handles smooth to the touch, a shining example of beauty. This is who we are. Treat us this way, and you'll be happy, and not so sore, either!"

Five

PLANTING FOR POLLINATORS

The sun is on fire
in the sky.
And in its warmth,
flowers open
in the garden.
And the butterfly
flutters by,
wings widespread.
It stops to feed
at the flower bed.

And on its favorite flower
the butterfly settles,
like two extra petals.

—*Stanley Cook*

Our beautiful garden sanctuary has taught us the value of planting for pollinators. When Steve and I began to develop the garden plan, we knew we wanted food and flowers—lots of flowers. We weren't even thinking about the pollinators at the time. All we knew was that we had lots of room to grow, and grow we did.

Our garden came to life one bed at a time. Here in the high desert, we're surrounded by open space with lots of beautiful rocks. Every day, Steve and I went scouting for rocks to use in the garden, loading them in the truck and bringing them home. Steve started creating unique beds, each rock lovingly placed to create a freestanding border. Once each bed was complete, we added leaves, compost, and various amendments and dug them into the native soil. Each new bed was watered and blessed into the garden. We began to fill the beds with herbs, vegetables, and flowers, creating a rainbow of color and fragrance. That's when the pollinators started showing up. There were bees in the herbs, butterflies on the zinnias, and then, the first iridescent flash of a hummingbird as it zoomed by! I put up a hummingbird feeder, and one or two birds started frequenting the "sugar tap." Pretty soon there were five, then ten, then twenty.

All were busy at the feeders and in the flowers we unknowingly planted for them. I started reading about hummingbirds so I could identify the different species we had in the garden as well as take notice of the flowers they frequented the most. We'd planted what we loved, and we'd created a beautiful buffet for the hummingbirds as well. I also noticed the garden was buzzing with bees, many species of bees. Of course, I recognized the honeybees, but there were others as well, and they were everywhere, especially among the herbs, the native plants, and the salvias. In just a short time, the whole garden had come alive with insect life. We'd created a beautiful home for so many just because we love flowers! The butterflies (sometimes known as flying flowers) started fluttering in. We live in an area full of open space and water, with lots of varieties of host plants available for the butterflies to lay their eggs in and for their future larvae (caterpillars) to eat. All we had to do was provide some butterfly favorites (which we did), and they came and blessed us with their grace and beauty.

Through the years, I've learned about the important role the pollinators play in our lives. It has been estimated that one out of every three bites of food comes to us through the work of animal pollinators and that 80 percent of the world's crop species require pollination to set seed. With pollinators' declining numbers, it's up to each of us to make choices in our lives that support them, particularly growing organically and creating specific habitats in which they can thrive. In doing this, your garden will not only be a beautiful place for you to enjoy but also benefit those that need it the most, our precious pollinators.

*People from a
planet without
flowers would
think we must be
mad with joy the
whole time to have
such things about us!*

—Iris Murdoch

ABOUT POLLINATORS

More than 200,000 individual animal species, through the use of varying strategies, help flowers to make more flowers. Bees forage among the flowers for pollen and nectar and then carry the pollen on their bodies, transferring it to the female parts of flowers, which then pollinate them. Slugs and snails smear pollen as they slide over flower clusters. Butterflies flutter from flower to flower to sip nectar, carrying a bit of the pollen with them because it sticks to their fuzzy bodies. The pollen is then released as they feed on each new flower. Flies and bees are considered to be the original pollinators, going back to when flowering plants first appeared 130 million years ago. Scientists have identified approximately twenty thousand distinct species of bee to date. One-fifth of those pollinate flowers in the United States, along with wasps, moths, butterflies, and hummingbirds. All feed on flowers and carry the pollen as they forage. Mosquitoes carry pollen for batches of orchids. Bats, with their diverse muzzles and tongues (which are adapted to tap differently shaped blossoms), are responsible for the pollination of 360 plants worldwide, and they are considered to be the second-most-important pollinator after wild bees. In the high mountains, flies are the main pollinators of the rugged plants that survive in the harsh alpine environment. Insects aren't the only animals that pollinate. Some nonflying mammals also help with this process. Sugar-loving opossums, lemurs in Madagascar, and some types of rainforest monkeys aid in pollination. With nimble hands, they tear open flower stalks, and the pollen sticks to their furry coats as they forage from flower to flower. There are even some lizards (such as geckos and skinks) that lap up nectar and pollen and then transport the stuff on their faces and feet as they move on.

Humans can also become pollinators by creating gardens that support these insects and animals in their daily environment. What pollinators need most is diversity of forage and a nontoxic environment for their foraging. Due to the prevalent use of intensive monoculture farming methods, building-development encroachment into habitat, and the widespread use of pesticides, herbicides, and GMOs containing these substances, many thousands of acres (at least) of wildflower habitat have been lost as a food source, contributing to the decline and loss of species. So, how do we turn this around? We can begin with our gardens and farms. How we grow food can be managed differently. By growing a variety of foods, not just one or two, and allowing some wildflowers to grow in our yards and on our farms (as was the practice before the widespread use of herbicides put an end to their natural way of growth), we can change the destructive patterns of growth that have brought us to this crisis. Commercial farms as well as home gardens need to adopt organic growing practices, and the use of GMO seeds and crops needs to be discontinued. More open space should be set aside as nature preserves in all parts of the world; this will help the migrating pollinators on their journeys around the globe. Individuals can assist by creating certified pollinator habitats at their homes, shopping organically, and boycotting products containing any GMO crops such as corn or soy. Each individual wildlife-friendly garden really makes a difference in the health of our pollinators. If you are starting a new garden or have an existing one, you can help the pollinators by planting a variety of wildlife-friendly plants, such as those containing ample nectar for hummingbirds, seeds for finches, and berries for waxwings and jays. You can add a water feature that will help the birds, insects, and frogs. You can put up birdseed feeders and organic sugar-water feeders. Sugar-water feeders not only attract hummingbirds but also draw in bees, orioles, and moths. There are so many ways to support the pollinators in our gardens, and in choosing to do so, you'll create a healthy, vibrant garden for everyone to enjoy. Right now, my garden is quite vibrant and bustling with activity; hummingbirds, sphinx moths, honeybees, bumblebees, carpenter bees, wasps, dragonflies, and butterflies are hovering and fluttering all about the flowers and sugar-water feeders. If every single home garden became a pollinator sanctuary like mine, we could really turn things around for the health of the planet and everyone on it. We can make a difference—one garden at a time. Provide the habitat and they will come, creating a magical garden of life for all to enjoy.

ABOUT HUMMINGBIRDS

Who doesn't marvel at the speed and agility of a hummingbird as it zooms by with wings humming and jewel-like colors sparkling in the sunshine? They are small in stature (two to twenty grams) but quite large in personality. It seems that they chase and squabble endlessly, whether protecting a feeder or a clump of wildflowers. Twittering and with wings buzzing, they zoom past us with a flash of color and an aerial dive that can leave us breathless. Unless they're nesting, they never seem to stop, from dawn to dusk. Even when perched, they're ever vigilant, watching for threat or opportunity. The most amazing thing of all is the way they fly. They have a unique method of rotating the entire wing with little or no wrist and elbow flexing. This makes them capable of forward, backward, and prolonged, hovering flight. Their body feathers are scale-like and highly iridescent, with some species so colorful that they're quite dazzling in the sunlight. Hummingbirds are native to the western hemisphere, and most of the species are found in the tropics. There are sixteen species that breed within the boundaries of the United States, and I happen to have the good fortune to live in an area of the West that is visited by six of those species. The hummingbirds I see are the Annas, Rufous, Costas, Black Chins, Broadtails, and Calliopes. The Annas is not a true migrant, as it resides in North America all year long, mostly along the western seaboard. The others can winter as far south as Mexico and breed as far north as Alaska. The Rufous have the most extensive migration in the West, wintering in the Mexican states of Zacatecas, Jalisco, Mexico, or Michoacán and spending their summers in British Columbia, up into Alaska. The Costas have a much shorter migration route, wintering in either Baja California, Arizona, or southern California. Their breeding range extends from southern and eastern California through Nevada and Utah. The Black Chin winters in southern California or Mexico and has a wide breeding range that includes a good portion of the West from Texas and up to British Columbia. The Broadtail winters in Central America and has a breeding range that includes Texas, Arizona, New Mexico, Utah, Colorado, Wyoming, and Nevada. The boundary of its western range reaches eastern California (where I live), so most California folks don't get to see the Broadtails.

The Calliopes are the smallest birds in North America. They are usually about two and a half inches to three inches long, in comparison to the Annas, which is four inches long and is North America's largest hummingbird. The Calliopes winter in Mexico and have a wide breeding range extending throughout Baja California, Utah, Wyoming, Oregon, Washington, British Columbia, and Alberta.

Most of the other hummingbirds that visit the United States are seen in New Mexico, Arizona, and Texas. There is only one hummingbird found east of the Mississippi River—the ruby-throated hummingbird. Its breeding range extends from Florida all the way to Canada.

Hummingbirds do not form bonds between male and female, and the male leaves all of the brooding and rearing of the young to the female. The males are always brightly colored to attract the females, whereas all female hummingbirds have plain, protective coloring. Female hummingbirds often choose their mate based on the abundance of food in his territory or by his display. The female often seeks out the male, and once she has found a prospective mate, he will do his best to impress her with his courtship behavior, which may include song, an exhibition of iridescent plumage, and dazzling aerial flights. If she chooses him, the mating is quick, and she will return to the nest she made prior to looking for a mate. Soon she lays two white, jelly-bean-sized eggs in a soft, flexible, and sturdy nest.

Hummingbird mothers generally sit on their eggs from 60 to 80 percent of each day. The incubation period is approximately fifteen to twenty-two days, and once the nestlings have hatched, the mother will diligently feed them until they've fledged. They can fledge (leave the nest) anywhere from twenty to thirty days. Once they've fledged, the mothers will often continue to preen (clean) and feed them. In learning how to feed themselves, the fledglings will try many types of flowers until they find those that produce plenty of nectar. Once they're sufficiently on their own, the mother will force them out of her territory, unless she happens to leave first. Young hummingbirds grow more rapidly when raised in areas in which there is an abundant food supply. Again, it's important for gardeners to provide a diverse plant pallet from which the hummingbirds can choose.

The hummingbirds will remain in their chosen territories until it's time for their southern migration. To prepare for this, they begin fattening up by increasing their food consumption. Each fall, I observe the increase of feeding activity, especially at the hummingbird feeders, to which they swarm like bees. The males generally leave before the females, and the juveniles leave last. (This is evidence that migration is instinctive, as they are not guided by their parents to their winter home.) During their fall migration, they will stop at frequent intervals to set up temporary feeding territories in gardens and among late-blooming wildflowers in open country along their route. Eventually, they end up at their winter destination. By contrast, the spring migration is urgent, as the birds hurry back to begin nesting, sometimes even before the spring wildflowers have blossomed. If there are no wildflowers, they'll survive on insects and, hopefully, find a home garden full of flowers and a sugar-water feeder.

Because of changing weather patterns, there are now hummingbird sightings in areas in which certain species have never been seen before. Also, with warmer winter temperatures now occurring in some parts of the United States, there are hummingbirds that have chosen to winter in those areas instead of heading further south to Mexico. This is where the hummingbird-friendly garden can play a key part in the support of overwintering hummingbirds, especially when the garden includes a sugar-water feeder. Because there aren't many wildflowers blooming in the United States in the winter (except for in south Florida), a sugar feeder can be a lifesaver for hungry, overwintering hummingbirds. If your garden includes plants that bloom early in the season, hummingbirds can receive nourishment from the nectar of those flowers as well. A hummer-friendly garden is also a boost for the long-distance travelers. The Rufous hummingbird travels a very long way, and your garden can be the perfect spot to rest and refuel on their long journey.

With the effects of climate change and urban sprawl and the widespread use of herbicides to kill "weeds," the diversity of wildflowers that hummingbirds have depended on for food during their migrations has been seriously compromised. This is a problem shared by many other pollinators as well. Our individual pollinator garden sanctuaries are needed more than ever to ensure pollinator survival. We can help them out, one garden at a time.

A pollinator garden full of hummingbird favorites is invaluable for migrating hummingbirds as well as for those that remain to raise their young. Here's a list for you of some of their favorite flowers. The more you plant, the richer the pallet they'll have to choose from.

Some Hummingbird Flower Favorites

- Salvia—all kinds (salvias grow on every continent except Antarctica)
- Penstemon—all kinds
- Zinnia
- *Fuchsia*
- Lavender
- Rosemary
- Larkspur
- Columbine
- Monarda—bee balm
- Scarlet runner beans
- Tithonia—Mexican sunflower
- Honeysuckle
- Hollyhocks
- Scarlet creeper vine
- Pink jasmine
- Mimulus—monkeyflower

Sugar-Water Feeders

Here's some helpful information for you on sugar-water feeders. I think hummingbird feeders are great! Even if you have an abundance of pollinator-friendly flowers in your garden, the hummingbirds and honeybees will still visit the feeders. They love them. The hummingbirds use them quite often, especially during migration season. It's a quick way for them to refuel and to fatten up their reserves. The honeybees often form bee clumps at the feeders—especially in my garden—and they seem to enjoy the opportunity to feed and socialize this way. The bees and hummers have a choice in my garden—feeders and flowers. They seem to like both, so that's what I give them. Everyone's happy.

I've found that the feeders I like the best are the glass models from Perky Pet. They offer different sizes, and they're easy to fill, easy to clean, durable, and relatively stable in the wind. Also, the hummingbirds and bees seem to prefer their feeder ports over other designs. Please don't buy the feeders advertised as bee proof. The bees still try to drink from them, and they get stuck and die in the process.

A common problem with hummingbird feeders is that, unfortunately, the sugar water attracts ants. There are ant deterrents on the market, and the best I've found are made by Perky Pet. They emit a pheromone that the ants don't like, and it's 100 percent effective. There are designs that use moats, which are problematic, as bees and hoverflies drown in the moats. I don't recommend them.

Please keep your feeders clean; the combination of sunlight and sugar grows mold, which isn't healthy for the hummers or the bees. I use a toothbrush and warm water to clean my feeders each time I refill them.

To make the "nectar" for the feeders, use a ratio of one cup sugar to four cups water. Use warm water, as this dissolves the sugar easier than cold water. If you choose to use organic cane sugar (highly recommended), you'll find that it dissolves much easier than the refined white sugar. Sugarcane is often a GMO crop and can be sprayed heavily with chemical pesticides, so it's best to use organic. It's more expensive, but it's worth the expense. Because the organic sugar is not refined, the sugar water has an amber color, which I like better than clear. Speaking of color, don't add any red food coloring to your feeders (or buy premade mix that contains red food coloring). The hummingbirds will find your feeder just fine without it, and they don't need the chemicals any more than you do.

When measuring the mix (sugar to water), use a small, glass measuring cup and mix it into a quart-size glass jar with a lid. Either use a spoon or shake the jar to help dissolve the sugar. Once it's dissolved, you can store the sugar water in the refrigerator for up to two weeks. Therefore, you'll have plenty on hand for hungry hummers, especially during migrating season.

Speaking of seasons, what do we do with the feeders when the weather turns cold? There's a myth that says leaving your feeders up will keep the hummingbirds from migrating, but it isn't true. They will always migrate if that's what their instincts tell them to do. If you are on the West Coast of the United States and you have Annas hummingbirds at your feeders, chances are they'll stay through the winter. They don't embark on a true migration, but they will travel short distances if their area has gotten too cold and they want to find a milder climate for the winter. Besides the Annas, there will possibly be fledglings that were born late in the season, and they'll remain until they've fattened up enough to make their first journey south. By leaving your feeders up, you'll help out the fledglings as well as any other migrating hummingbirds passing through your area. Migrating monarch and Painted Lady butterflies will also enjoy the feeders on their travels, and honeybees will feed on sunny days.

If you live in an area with cold autumns and winters, you can put a piece of insulation around the glass part of the feeder. Lined bubble wrap works beautifully for this. Cut it to size to fit the feeder, and cut out a small, vertical window so you can see how much sugar water is in the feeder. Wrap the insulation around the feeder, fastening it with a piece of packaging tape. The insulation will keep the sugar water in liquid form even when the night temperature drops below freezing. On really cold nights you can bring the feeders in and then hang them out in the morning. The hummers and occasional honeybees will enjoy the late-season nourishment.

If your area experiences really cold winters, eventually the hummingbirds will migrate to warmer climates and you can remove your feeders for the season. Remember to scrub them well and let them dry before storage. When the weather begins to warm up in late winter or early spring, depending on where you live, you can put them back out again (using the insulation if you need to).

Sugar-water feeders are a great source of energy for early-season arrivals, especially if there aren't many flowers blooming at that time. These days, with so much development encroaching on the wild spaces, there's not as much forage available for migrating hummingbirds. A sugar-water feeder can be just what they need to refuel for their travels. And that's a good thing.

ABOUT BUTTERFLIES

Butterflies are beautiful flying insects with large wings covered in colorful iridescent scales in overlapping rows. They are true sun-loving creatures, as they can fly only if their body temperature is at or above 86°F. They must warm themselves up in cool weather before they can fly. The speed they fly at varies among butterfly species. Slow-flying butterflies (such as the monarch) fly, or flutter, about five miles per hour, whereas the fastest butterflies (some skippers) can fly at about thirty miles per hour or faster.

Butterflies and moths belong to the order Lepidoptera. There are at least 150,000 different species of butterflies and moths worldwide, and of that amount, 28,000 are butterflies; the rest are moths. The earliest butterfly fossils are from the early cretaceous period, about 130 million years ago. Their development is closely linked to the evolution of flowering plants, since both caterpillars and adult butterflies feed on flowering plants and the adults are important pollinators for flowering plants.

The order Lepidoptera includes a wide array of butterflies and moths, all unique in their wing colors and designs. *Lepides* is Greek for "scales," and *plera* means "wing." Their scaled wings are different from the wings of any other insects. They are actually formed of tiny overlapping pieces of chitin (a common building material for animal bodies), which are outgrowths of their body wall. They are often different colors on the top and bottom, and they often shine in the sunlight.

The most fascinating thing about the butterflies and the moths is their process of metamorphosis. They go through four different life stages to complete this process—the egg, the larvae, the pupa, and, finally, the adult butterfly or moth. The female lays her cluster of eggs on or underneath a leaf on a specific host plant. The eggs then hatch, and the larvae (caterpillars) spend their time constantly eating the host plant's leaves or flowers. The caterpillar molts (sheds its skin) several times until the last molt, at which point it enters the pupa (chrysalis) stage. Inside the chrysalis, the pupa is growing into an adult butterfly. When it is fully formed, it emerges from its chamber by using its body to push against the wall of the chrysalis until it tears open. Once the butterfly has emerged, it begins to pump liquid into its damp vein wings in order to inflate them. The butterfly is now ready to begin its new life as a beautiful flying creature. It can eat only liquids, which it does by sipping nectar through its proboscis, a long flexible "tongue" that uncoils to sip food and coils up again into a spiral when not in use.

Butterflies visit many flowers for nectar, but there are certain favorites they frequent the most. Often these are flowers that are found in small, tight clusters, such as yarrow or scabiosa. They also love zinnias and Echinaceas, which have brightly colored petals (known as bracts) surrounding the true golden clusters of flowers nestled in the center of the bracts.

There are many butterflies that migrate. Even though there might be a plentiful food source available, they will still travel when it's time to go. Many butterflies that migrate do so in order to avoid adverse environmental conditions, particularly cold weather. Some migrate relatively short distances, such as the painted lady, red admiral, and common buckeye. The monarch butterflies, however, undertake a much longer migration, sometimes traveling thousands of miles. They accomplish this in successive stages; it often takes three generations (or more) to complete the migration. Females lay their eggs along the migratory route, so each generation continues on from where the previous generation completed its part of the journey.

The life span of the adult monarch varies depending on the season in which it emerged from the pupa and whether it belongs to a migratory group of monarchs. Adults that emerged in early summer have the shortest life spans and live for about two to five weeks. Those that emerged in late summer survive the winter months by traveling to a warmer climate and hibernating for the winter. They return to the same trees every year. There have been sanctuaries created to protect hibernating monarchs west of the Rocky Mountains in areas such as Santa Cruz, Santa Barbara, and Pacific Grove, California. These monarchs live a much longer life, about eight to nine months. Some groups of monarchs east of the Rocky Mountains migrate over two thousand miles from August through October. They fly from Canada and the United States to overwinter in the transvolcanic mountains of central Mexico.

The monarch butterfly is found all around the world in subtropical to tropical areas. It favors open habitat such as meadows, fields, marshes, and gardens. An area in which its host plant, milkweed, is plentiful allows the monarch to proliferate, and this area can serve as an important monarch butterfly sanctuary.

Since most species of butterflies use the wild spaces in nature to lay their eggs and then feed the caterpillars from the variety of plants that grow in these wild spaces, it's essential that we keep our wildlands in their natural state. Unfortunately, butterfly numbers have been declining from the widespread use of pesticides and herbicides and from urban sprawl. Open flower fields in which butterflies have foraged for years are being cut down or poisoned, and many habitats that served as food for the larva (caterpillars) have met the same fate. The monarchs that depend on wildflower nectar along their long migratory route are in serious jeopardy. If we want to save these pollinators, we need to stop the use of poisons, which do not discriminate in the species of victims they destroy. We need to allow for more diversity of flowering plants in our environment, which includes our farms, parks, yards, and gardens. We can create a butterfly habitat at home by providing them with food (flowers), water, shelter, and host plants on which they can lay their eggs. In this way, we are meeting their needs at each stage of life, from egg to larva to pupa to adulthood.

The plants you choose for your butterfly garden will be in two categories. One is the host plant (which are species specific) on which the butterfly will lay its eggs and from which it will provide food for the caterpillar. (An example is milkweed for the monarchs.) The other includes all the nectar plants that will feed the adult butterfly. It's important to consider providing for some of the other needs of butterflies when creating your butterfly garden. These needs include sunlight (which they need to regulate body temperature), a succession of blooming flowers throughout the gardening season (so they have a steady supply of nectar), a shallow water feature from which they can drink, and shady areas in which they can cool off if your garden is hot in the summer. If you live in a rural area, chances are the open space will include some of the host plants required to feed a variety of butterfly species larva. In this case, your butterfly garden need only be a beautiful bouquet of their favorite flowers for nectar.

But if you live in an area in which various butterfly host plants aren't growing close by, then you'll need to provide some host plants in your garden. Keep in mind that these plants are *host* plants and that the caterpillars are going to eat them. Also, pruning is not recommended, as you might be cutting back stems with precious eggs attached to the leaves. So, you'll need to leave the host plants alone except for irrigation. Accept the fact that they might get pretty ragged looking. It's worth it, though, because watching the whole process is quite amazing, and knowing that you're supporting the lives of these special creatures is a beautiful thing indeed.

Here's a list of host plants and the caterpillars that feed on them as well as of favorite butterfly flowers. This will give you a good start on creating a wonderful butterfly sanctuary.

Common Butterflies and Their Host Plants

- Anise swallowtail—anise, fennel, carrots, parsley
- Black swallowtail—parsley, carrots
- Painted lady—daisy family, especially thistles
- Gulf fritillary and zebras—passionflower leaves
- Greater and lesser fritillaries—violets
- Red admiral—nettles
- Mourning cloak—elms, willows, poplar
- Cloudless sulphur—wild *Senna*
- Monarch—milkweed
- Buckeye—plantain
- West Coast lady—mallows
- Fawn—birch alders
- Zephyr—elm and currant
- Comma—nettles, hops
- Viceroy—willow and poplar
- California sister—live oak
- Silver spotted skipper—wisteria, locust
- Marine blue—buds and blossoms of wisteria, alfalfa, locoweed, and legumes
- Field crescent—asters

Some Butterfly Flower Favorites

- Echinacea
- Zinnia
- Butterfly bush
- Scabiosa
- Jupiter's Beard
- Self-heal
- Rosemary
- Clover
- Daisy family
- Salvia family
- Tithonia—Mexican sunflower
- Milkweeds
- Pentas
- Passionflower
- Fruit-tree blossoms: apricots, plums, and so on
- Yarrow

ABOUT BEES

Bees are important indicators of the health of the environment. When something is wrong with the bees, something is wrong with the health and balance of our planet.

Bees belong to the insect order Hymenoptera, along with wasps, ants, and sawflies. There are about twenty-five thousand known species of bees in the world. The majority of bees are actually solitary species. They don't live together in social colonies as honeybees and bumblebees do; instead they live alone, although some may build their nests close to each other. Depending on the species, bees may nest in the ground or in cavities (such as tree trunks or crevices in buildings). Some species nest on the surface of the ground, such as in clumps of grass.

Social bees have different life spans depending on the kind of bee and its role within the colony. The life span of honeybees, for example, is determined by the role of the individual bee as well as the time of year it was born. A honeybee queen can live for three to four years as long as she is free from disease. Workers raised during spring or summer may live from six to seven weeks. Their lives are busy with lots of hungry larvae to feed and honeycomb to be produced. They are busy collecting nectar and pollen to feed the colony. Those raised in autumn don't have to care for larvae because the queen stops producing eggs. Part of the colony often leaves in a swarm in fall to form a new colony with a new queen. The workers that remain will huddle together around their queen in order to keep warm during the winter. They will be ready to forage again in early spring. In my garden, the sugar-water feeders continue to feed the Annas hummingbirds throughout the winter, and on warm, sunny days, the bees will venture out to forage at the feeders as well. When the rosemary and crocus begin to bloom in early February, the bees add that to their palette and their pollinating season begins anew.

With bumblebees, the new queens emerge in late summer or early autumn. After mating, they will forage to store their fat reserves, which will carry them through their winter hibernation. Early the next spring, the new queens emerge to establish their new colonies. (The colonies that raised these queens will have died before the winter began.) Each queen will choose a nest site, and once she has found her place, she will build a little wax cup inside the nest, which she fills with nectar to sustain her while she incubates her eggs. She will also create a further wax cell in which she'll deposit a mound of pollen. Then she'll lay her eggs on top of it. She incubates her eggs by lying on top of them and vibrating her flight muscles, which generates heat up to 85°F. After four days, the eggs hatch; the larvae emerge looking like little maggots. They'll shed their skin three times in two weeks, and then they'll produce silken cocoons and pupate. While in their cocoons, they'll shed their skin one more time and undergo metamorphosis.

It takes two weeks for the grublike larvae to transform into young bumblebees, biting their way out of their cocoons. The first to emerge are young female worker bees. Meanwhile, the queen has laid more eggs, and the emerging workers will assist in rearing the rest of the brood. Some workers will begin to go out and forage for pollen and nectar. A bumblebee colony usually consists of around 120 to 200 bees, sometimes more. At some point, the queen stops producing workers and switches to rearing males and young queens. The males leave the nest to search for mating opportunities, and the young queens leave the nest to mate and hibernate for the winter, reemerging in spring to establish new colonies of their own.

Bees and other insects pollinate plants as they forage on the flowers. Honeybees gather pollen and nectar and return to their hives, transferring pollen from one flower to another. Pollen gathered from the male part of the flower, known as the anther, sticks to the honeybee's fuzzy body and is transferred onto the stigma—the female part—of the next flower. The stigma is often sticky, making it easier for the pollen to remain in place.

Bumblebees are also excellent plant pollinators. Their coats are fuzzy—even more so than honeybees—which means they easily pick up pollen and transfer it to other plants. They forage through a long season in temperate climates, so they're important pollinators of early- and late-season crops and wildflowers. Bumblebees are capable of "buzz pollination." They place their thorax (upper body) close to the anthers of a flower and vibrate their flight muscles. The vibration shakes the pollen from the anthers, which is helpful for pollinating those plants, such as kiwis, blueberries, and strawberries, that require help to shake loose their pollen.

Solitary bees are also important pollinators. There are some plants and crops that are pollinated only by wild bees and other pollinators such as wasps and flies. Wild bees have long tongues, so deep and "complicated" flowers are pollinated by wild bees, especially bumblebees.

Pollen is crucial for honeybee brood development and is made into bee bread. The pollen is mixed with water and nectar from the bees' mouths, which causes the pollen granules to grow. The bee bread is stored in honeycombs and is used by all members of the colony, although it's especially good for the baby bee's development and growth. The bee bread even helps to add a certain amount of structural integrity to the honeycomb. All pollen collected by insects is of high nutritional value—more so than pollen carried by the wind—so flowers that contain this pollen have great appeal to the insects as a food source.

Bees are outstanding pollinators generally, but some bees are better suited for pollinating certain plants than are other bees. This depends on the bee's method of collecting pollen, the body shape of the bee and the flower, and the tongue length of the bee (the longer the tongue, the deeper the flowers they can feed from).

All bees require a diet of both pollen and nectar. Pollen provides them with vital protein and fats while nectar provides a complex range of sugars for energy. In the honeybee hive, the nectar that is gathered is passed from the foraging worker bees to worker house bees, who deposit it into honeycomb cells. After a process of fanning and evaporation, the nectar will turn into honey, and it will be capped over with wax by the bees. This provides a winter food source for the entire colony to dip into when they are unable to forage outside the hive for food.

All bee species, honeybees and wild bees, are important pollinators, and they're having a hard time as their numbers continue to decline. If we make good life choices with the pollinators in mind, the quality of our lives will improve, and collectively, the quality of life for the pollinators will improve as well. Our home gardens can become the little spot of paradise the bees need to thrive. Grow organically and provide a diverse pallet of flowers for them to forage on through all the seasons, including early spring and late into fall. Make an effort to purchase plants, bulbs, and seeds that are free of neonicotinoids and systemic insecticides. (These are used widely in Holland, so avoid purchasing bulbs and plants from that country.) Create nest sites for wild bees, such as bundles of hollow canes for cavity nesters, and so on. If you are interested in beekeeping, I suggest you check out the website of an organic beekeeper named Randy Sue Collins. Her website will provide you with all the information you'll need to get started with organic beekeeping. She's also the creator of a wonderful beehive design that she calls the Hex Hive. You can contact Randy at randysuebeehaven.wordpress.com. She also has a wealth of information on another website: organicbeekeeping101.com.

MEET SOME OF THE WILD BEES

There are many delightful wild bees that will take up residence in a bee-friendly garden. I'm going to include a brief description of some of them here to give you a better understanding of who they are and the vital part they play in the garden and in the rest of nature as well.

Mason Bees. Mason bees use mud in the construction of their nests. They are cavity-nesting bees, and once a brood cell has been made, mud is used to make partitions between each individual cell. The adults emerge in spring; the males are first, waiting to mate. After mating, the males die and the female seeks a suitable location for her nest. She provides pollen and nectar in each cell for a single larva; eggs destined to become females are laid toward the back, and males are toward the front. They'll make anywhere from four to six cells (sometimes ten), and four to five similar nests may be completed in a season. There will be one generation per year. Masons provide an excellent pollination service, especially in fruit orchards, so you can encourage them to set up home by purchasing a ready-made mason-bee home or making one yourself. A bundle of hollow canes or an untreated log drilled with holes (one centimeter in diameter or less—ten centimeters long) will provide a good home for them.

Leafcutter Bees. These are also cavity nesters, like mason bees. Once a suitable spot has been found, they will build cells using pieces of a leaf they have gathered to make a cylindrical cavity. Each cell is sealed up with a little segment of the leaf; leafcutter bees always cut away segments of leaf in a very neat fashion. The segment of leaf is grasped and carried below the body of the bee and transported to the nest. The female will lay a single egg in each cell and supply it with pollen, on which the larva feeds once it hatches. The larva will develop inside the cell, overwinter, and emerge as an adult the following spring or early summer. Leafcutter bees don't have pollen baskets on their hind legs with which to transport the pollen back to the nest (that's a honeybee trait). Instead, they collect pollen on hairs on the underside of their abdomens.

You can provide a similar home for leafcutter bees as for mason bees. Both mason and leafcutter bees prefer their homes to have a southern exposure for warmth, and make sure the holes in the canes or log are one centimeter—if they're too small, other insects such as ladybugs will use them instead (which isn't a bad thing—you can make homes for both).

Carpenter Bees. These bees make their nests by boring holes in wood. They use small amounts of wood chips to form partitions between the cells, in which they lay their eggs. Although solitary, some species of carpenter-bee females may live alongside their sisters or daughters, thus forming a basic social group. Carpenter bees emerge from hibernation in the spring. After mating, the female constructs her nest alone and lays her eggs within a series of small cells, each supplied with a ball of pollen on which the larvae feed.

The larvae emerge as adults in late summer and forage until late fall, hibernating until the following year. Carpenter bees are more inclined to make their nests in rotting, old, or damaged wood. As long as home-owners maintain their woodwork, keeping it well painted and in good condition, there won't be a problem with carpenter bees. They are not out to make work for themselves by selecting hard, painted wood that is difficult for them to bore into.

Mining Bees. They are one of the largest groups of solitary bees, consisting of over 1,300 known species across the world. They prefer to build nests in sandy soil, each nest consisting of one small, main tunnel with perhaps five or so branches, each of which contains an egg cell. They emerge in spring and mate, and like other female solitary bees, the female mining bee will set about making egg cells, laying an egg in each cell and providing both pollen and nectar on which the individual larva can feed. Each individual egg cell is made, provisioned, and then sealed up before the next cell is made. Usually about five eggs are laid. The adults are active for about six to eight weeks of the year, and the new adults that emerge will hibernate over the winter, reemerging in spring. A nest may be reoccupied year after year if undisturbed.

Wool Carder Bees. This bee has striking yellow and black markings and, at first glance, can be easily mis-taken for a wasp. This bee collects, or cards, the hairs from plants and uses these to line the egg cells. They create their nests in holes, hollow stems, and crevices, similar to mason and leafcutter bees. They raise a single generation of offspring each year. The males are actually territorial; they are protective of their chosen patches of flowers and, like hummingbirds, will defend their territories from intruders (that is, other insects). They are attracted to a large variety of flowers for general foraging as well as specific plants for their hairs. Lamb's ear is a wool carder bee favorite.

In closing, it's really time we learn to treat our honeybees in a gentle and respectful manner, as they provide us with so much. It's also time we learn to honor our wild bees too. We need to create safe habitats for all bees to forage and to flourish. If each one of us gardeners all across the world created bee-haven gardens, there's a good chance that our bees—both wild and domesticated—will continue to bless our planet for many years to come. It's all up to us.

Bee Flower Favorites

- Salvia family
- Herbs—borage, rosemary, mint, basil, thyme, sage, and so on
- Amaranth
- Scabiosa
- Monarda—bee balm
- Roses
- Dahlias
- Cactus flowers
- Zinnias
- Lavender
- Lamb's ear
- Vegetable garden flowers—especially squash blossoms, onion flowers, and carrot flowers
- Hollyhocks
- Columbines
- Penstemons
- Fruit-tree blossoms—pear, plum, peach, and so on

Plant	Bee	Butterfly	Hummingbird
Amaranth	Yes		
Butterfly bush		Yes	
Cactus flowers	Yes		
Clover		Yes	
Columbines	Yes		Yes
Dahlia	Yes		
Daisy family		Yes	
Echinacea		Yes	
Fruit-tree blossoms	Yes	Yes	
Fuchsias			Yes
Herbs	Yes		
Hollyhocks	Yes		Yes
Honeysuckle			Yes
Jupiter's beard		Yes	
Lamb's ear	Yes		
Larkspur			Yes
Lavender	Yes		Yes
Milkweeds		Yes	
Milulus, monkeyflowers			Yes
Monarda—bee balm	Yes		Yes
Passionflower			

Penstemons	Yes		Yes
Pentas		Yes	
Pink jasmine			Yes
Rosemary	Yes	Yes	Yes
Roses	Yes		
Saliva family	Yes	Yes	Yes
Scabiosa	Yes	Yes	
Scarlet creeper vine			Yes
Scarlet runner beans			Yes
Tithonia, Mexican sunflower		Yes	Yes
Vegetable garden flowers	Yes		
Yarrow		Yes	
Zinnias	Yes	Yes	Yes

A Conversation with Bees, Part 1 (Bakersfield, California)
by Mary Tannheimer

I had three meetings with a group of bees brought by truck to Bishop from Bakersfield, and I set up with their boxes in the sage and rabbitbrush along a dirt road near the Owens River. I walk on that road often in the morning, and I noticed the bee traffic on the bushes before I got near the boxes. I did not want to get close enough to interfere with the flight paths in and out, so I simply observed the bustle and said hello. Later in the afternoon I returned in my truck, parked nearby facing the boxes, and began a conversation.

Bees (in my face): "Who are you?"
Mary: "My friend and I are writing a book, and we would like to know about your life here in the boxes so we can put your experiences in the book."
Bees: "It's not good for us!"
Bees (in my face): "We don't trust you!"
Mary: "All people aren't like the ones you're with."
Bees: "Then why don't you *do* something?"
Mary: "We're *trying* to do something!"
Bees (angry): "It *better* do something!"

Finally, they began to speak.

"We are always afraid. This is how we grow up [with no choice, as victims]. We are not violent creatures but live with large amounts of violence, and so we developed a potent sting and a bad attitude for survival's sake. You played with us and made us weak and vulnerable. Some of us are hopeless, and some are angry about this. Some (very few, but some) have a positive attitude, usually young ones, like your children. It is beaten out of us (mostly) by the time we are adults (just like you—interesting comparison, huh?). Why are we all victims? Because this is a planet of victimhood. It is a lesson for developing consciousness. Here is another—do not be careless with what you create. It needs your love and attention to flourish. It is not fair to create and then leave creation behind unattended. This creates unresolved fear and confusion. Only create what you can care for—no more. This is a lesson we know well, but your kind hasn't understood it sufficiently yet. This is a basic concept in our hive; our lives revolve around it. Even though there are so many of us, we still know that we are all loved and cared for throughout our seemingly short lives. You do not practice this and therefore have much unnecessary suffering in your lives, from your births onward. This lack of wisdom has helped many hurtful behaviors flourish among humans, and our treatment is an outgrowth of this.

"We have cities like you, with streets like you and communities of like-minded individuals. We are usually grouped by what we eat, and we share our lives in as much happiness as we can muster before you destroy our homes and loot our property. We start over again and again but are never secure in our future. We never know when you will intrude and take us from ourselves, so we live in the moment, often frantically trying to pack in the most we can before you come again. Inside the hive, we rest and regain control with our friends. It is very hard on us. Compare this to your lives. We are learning the same lessons here about power and powerlessness. Think about your life and how much others take from you without your consent. We [bees and people] are here to learn that this is detrimental to our spirit health, and there are better ways to go."

Now the queens speak up.

Queens: "We have been listening. We are glad you came."
Mary: "This is going in a book for everyone to read."
Queens: "We know this, and we will tell the truth of our lives here in these boxes. It is not necessarily so in other places [on Earth and dimensionally]. We are here to create life. We love our creations—our children—and it makes our hearts ache to watch them suffer and die in such hopelessness and fear."
Mary: "Why do you do it then?"
Queens: "Someone must do it, or this planet will die. That is how important we are. That is why we are so many. It takes multitudes to keep things running. We fulfill our duties to our beloved planet, but our hearts are filled with sorrow at your callousness toward this beautiful and loving Earth, our planet, your home and all of ours—plants, animals, insects, rocks, air, water. We try to show you a different way, a loving way, a way without hatred—an emotion you so heartily embrace. There is a better way—one of compassion and sharing, of companionship and laughter—in which all are honored for their uniqueness. You can celebrate uniqueness even though you share a common goal—unity of purpose toward a project, with love and attention to *all* aspects of the creative process. Each gives his or her unique best for the common good. None need suffer, for there is enough for all. Attention and care to the resources of life make sure there is enough for all, because *all* are important and none are created carelessly. Your Buddha talks of mindfulness. Are you mindful? We are, even in our weakened state. We are always mindful, except when hit with such violent thoughts that some of our children sometimes forget. We as queens never forget. Our memory stretches

into infinity, reaching the source of all life. It is our responsibility as parents to feed this to our young, and we do, literally, in our food, so they have a real awareness of their importance to the whole and their responsibility to protecting and maintaining their beautiful, loving planet—our gorgeous Earth. Do you do this with *your* children, or do you teach them to forget their true heritage from the stars? We are all holy, every being on this planet. We all came from the same source. There is only One, and it is expressed uniquely in each of us. We all have great intrinsic value in the scheme of things. Do you act that way? Do you live your own importance with love and care? We do. Your peoples are finally beginning to see the results of careless, mindless creation. It shows in the ineffectiveness of your lives—the powerlessness you feel, the violence you receive from others, the victimhood you are still trapped in. When will you stand up for yourselves in love and strength and say, 'Enough. No more. My life is more valuable than this charade. I am more than this and I *will* become it!' Your lives would change in an instant, and this lovely creation called Earth would be an instant heaven. These things are not difficult. It is your belief in victimhood that makes them seem insurmountable. They are *not*!

"We have tried to show you how cooperation and caring can make a different world, but over the ages, we have fallen some ourselves. Fear is a *great* illusion, wielded by some as a sword of Damocles to keep others enslaved in another's movie. We are leaving in large groups to revitalize our lineages and spirit forms, to be awake and ready for the new world of peace that is on the verge of appearing. You have much work to do within yourselves to match the work being done by the rest of the earthly species that wish to live in this new world. Remember, creation by default will never be successful. It is careless by nature, and only weakness will result from carelessness.

"We thank you for your attention and hope you will look deeper at yourselves and your lives. We send you blessings from the Source, the one that lives inside each of you. Wake up to yourselves. It is beautiful inside each of you. Move away the darkness and fear, and shine forth as the beautiful beings you are. You are *so* gorgeous when you shine, like golden, glowing flowers, and we *know* flowers! Blessings to you. Smile at us when we fly by. We send you kisses like we kiss the flowers. You can do it. We are here for you, all of us, and there are billions of us, so never feel alone or lost. We love you all so much, because we love beauty. Come again and talk. We wait for you. Each of you."

I felt them kissing my face, and then they were gone.

A Conversation with Bees, Part 2

Mary: "Good morning to all of you! Will you speak more to me about your lives?"

Many voices: "Good morning! We are glad you have come again! Our dialogue is very important, and we want to keep it going, for the answers are near."

Mary: "I have had much to think about since we spoke last and am wondering what you can propose to us as solutions to the approaching disaster that we created with our unconscious behaviors."

Many voices speak among themselves, and then one is prominent: "We will let our queens speak to answer this, as they have this in front of them always, until their deaths."

One voice then speaks.

"When my children come crying back to me (plural), of course I think of solutions. Wouldn't you? We have access to larger ways of thinking, whereas you have shut yourselves off from experiencing difference, so you have closed your informational channels. What has it done for you? Made a mess, actually. Our predicament is directly related to yours, as we are all one in this planetary experience. Loving yourselves would be a good thing for all of us here on Earth. How about it? You are wonderful creatures, creative and true yet so lost. Are you happy being lost, or would you be happier being found? We think the latter. We love you so, as we do our children, and it pains us to see you suffer like you do—so lost when the solution is right in front of you. Happiness is what you make it."

Mary: "How can humans have honey yet still allow coexistence?"

Queen: "Look at our lives in our reality, not yours. Make the conjoining of our [human and bee] efforts as close to bee reality as is feasible. Do we live in square boxes in our world? Do we all eat the same food all the time, or do our communities swap territories? We have fun and excitement on our journeys in our world. Do you, or do you worry about your lives on your travels? You say, "How will I exist if I stop and smell the roses?" We liken your lives to those of the ants, who truly do have a very limited view of the world, as they walk on the ground and rarely seem to look up. Sound familiar?"

Mary: "I am having trouble staying focused in this conversation."

Queen: "That's because the solutions seem hard to you humans. Greed, power, and fear run in the same pack, and humans are running with that pack at this time. Let go of these, and answers come quickly and easily. You will be surprised at the changes that come in short periods of time.

"We see hexagonal domes for houses, with ports for entry and exit. Designate areas for bee housing only and human honey consumption only. Don't mix the two. *Many* of us will choose to serve you if we are *asked*. Always *ask* before you make decisions with our lives, just as you want to be asked about your lives. Allow us to choose our breeding facilities for royalty, and do *not* interrupt our processes. After these are in place, *ask* for our commitments to you in specific requests, so we may confidently know your needs. Honey is good for all humans (even those with allergies, which are curable in all cases), and we are happy to oblige your scavenging as long as it is done with care for our lives. Greed is an overwhelming factor in this scavenging on Earth today. This form of scavenging needs to change into interspecies cooperation. There is enough to go around. Hoarding is not necessary. Brutality is not necessary. Unconsciousness is no longer productive to any life on this planet. Could you live if someone else did to you what you have done to us? Actually, there *are* those on your planet who are doing to you what you have done to us, and you have *allowed* it! We are all reflections of each other in this world. Imagine how wonderful our lives could all be if we simply loved and allowed each other to be the true spark that drives each of us! Heaven on Earth, as we have said. Instantly.

"Science has laughed and has obscured our truth by classifying and relegating us to a lesser form of being, all out of fear and misinformation propagated by those who are much more fearful than will be acknowledged. Yet these people have secured for themselves vast kingdoms of power. This is useless and damaging. Science has its place, but until it acquires a heart, its function is juvenile and quite useless. Each of you has power far greater than you admit, and if you seize your own power and walk your own path, you truly become immortal. What a glorious way to participate in the earthly experience, where all is done in cocreative harmony! We acknowledge our differences but create a balanced life for all those involved. Obviously for most of you, this will be a process, one truly attainable if grasped and trusted without letting go. It *can* be done. We can live and sustain each other without harm or ugliness. The other species on Earth will support you. Look at your fragile efforts to amend your actions. Millions of humans *do* care and *can* love in harmony. The rest are simply uneducated. They can relearn to love!

"The bottom line (what a phrase—so expressive of the weakness of your prevailing value system!) is: let us live as we will, and create spaces for us in your lives that we can inhabit as though they were ours.

This gives us the freedom to make choices for *everyone's* benefit, both bee and human, without anxiety or stress. Talk with us, share your mealtimes with us, plant your gardens with us, and raise your children with us, and we will share ourselves like you have never imagined possible. Love and joy are ours to share with you, and we are *so* waiting to do so. We love you all. You are so beautiful and caring at your core. We want to share our lives with you, for all of us will become the glorious sparks of creation we were meant to be.

"Enough for now. Do you wish to know anything else?"

Mary: "What meaning does the mixing with African bees have in your lives?"

Queen: "Many European bee colonies are hybridizing with our African cousins. It is impossible to keep Africans out anymore. The wild spirit is necessary to rebuild the bee spirit that has been virtually obliterated on Earth through human meddling. Everyone wants to play God so they feel important, but they won't look at themselves to actually develop their "God nature." Careless, haphazard creation is doomed to failure and causes unnecessary suffering. There is much to learn here for you.

"The intent of the African hybrid-bee developers was to do this exact thing (strengthen the breed), but they were poorly informed. They botched the project. Many bees escaped the "factory" [the bees used this word to describe the project] and went rogue. This was actually a good thing, for the African's spirit is so strong it cannot be defeated. This has created a "hero" culture for European bees, and the spirit is passed on more easily through desire and a form of worship. (Although worship isn't actually healthy, because it increases the desire's power exponentially.) This is occurring on the creation levels, so physicality is the last to show it, thus making it hard for humans to see. This is happening with all Earth's life-forms. Throngs are waiting entrance to the new world with much stronger and more balanced blueprints for living.

"We have spoken enough on these things now. We thank you for listening to our side of the dialogue. We much appreciate your attention to our concerns. Thank-you for your time."

I cried a little with all of this, and many bees said, "Don't cry. Let us kiss your face and help you move away from your sorrow. It's why we were made—to kiss the faces of the Earth."

A Conversation with Bees, Part 3

Sunday, November 8, 2014

Bees: "So you've come back!"
Mary: "Yes, this will be my last time before you go."
Bees: "We have so enjoyed talking with you."
Other bees: "This [outdoors] is the best part of our lives. It's almost like we're wild again."
Mary: "You look so content in your privacy."
Bees: "We really enjoy it so much. It connects us back to home."
Mary: "You said once that your life may not be the way of other bees. What does that mean?"

In my mind, bees come up to my face, drip some honey on my tongue, and kiss me.

Bees: "The flowers are almost gone. We will be leaving soon."
Queen: "Our life is a dreary one, but it's one we have chosen. This life furthers our informational channels so that those who come behind can make better, more appropriate choices for their lives. We have come to you today to share the reason we have made these current choices. We are a mirror to you. We want you to see how you have circumscribed your lives by the choices you've made. You have seen us as cute and fuzzy, a kind of toy to play with. You say, "Maybe we'll do this with you, or maybe we'll do that with you," just playing with us like children do. Some of you are bullies to us, and some are kinder, but it's all in a sense of unconscious manipulation. This is how you have been treated as a species, so it's all you know. You can relearn the truths you have misplaced. The animal kingdom can teach you that. As there are many kinds of people, so there are many kinds of animals. We all gravitate to each other, so we can all learn about life. It is time to wake up now to yourselves and the kind, loving beings you truly are. Your masters think they can outwit us [the animals and insects], but we are too many and too varied to succumb to useless games. Even those who have closed to us are still affected. The men who wear the suits, pull us out of the boxes, and smash us are exactly the same as those of us who are smashed. They are used for the skills they have to offer and then tossed aside for new fodder. They don't see it that way. They are providing for their families in the best ways they understand, but their understanding is very limited. Like attracts like, so this brutal behavior has been a constant in their growing up (we never stop growing up). They believe it to be necessary and appropriate.

When one is raised with brutality, it is all one knows. The pathways in the brain can be rerouted to a kinder way. It is all a process. Life is built on life, so change is incremental but not necessarily in small increments. We feed our children love, so they will feed their children love. It goes on and on and expands out to the plants we touch, the trees we live in and land on, and even the people we sting. Our vital truth touches everything. That is why we are so many. Love goes wherever we go, and we go *everywhere*! We touch all hearts to wake them up to the truth of Love. Love is insurmountable. Even where we have left completely, the people have understood our love and try to copy our actions in their plant worlds. They have understood the need for love in relation to others. It may appear selfish, as in, "We can't live without food," but this is an appearance only. The truth has hit home, and the understanding of the need for active love stands behind their actions. Because we are perceived as cute and fuzzy, our purposes and activities in love are not refused but sought after in gratitude and acceptance. This has been our plan from the beginning and is why the new world will succeed. Please don't spend time sorrowing over what is. Rejoice and clap over what is coming. Release yourselves from your white bee suits and dance and sing at our sides. Your masters know the new world is at hand and their power structure is falling, so be glad for yourselves. Look up! See the sky and the flowers all around you. Each of you is a flower on the stem of humanity. Help each other bloom into the glorious colors each of you wears. Neither our travails nor yours are in vain when we all, each of us, human and bee, stand up and work together for the advancement of Love. The most inconscient still feels the touch of Love. That is why we send ourselves to the boxes. That is why you send yourselves to the slums and the factories and the prisons and the slaughterhouses. It opens the doors to change. Love penetrates all, visibly or invisibly, and the brave souls who choose to mask their divinity and enter the halls of unconsciousness still have the truth in their hearts. Remember that. Appearances are utterly deceiving, yet that is your present standard of achievement. Loosen your bonds of unconsciousness, and let your freedom begin! Move out of your boxes, and fly free in the glory of your own unique selves. Do not judge or ridicule. Allow all their own distinctions and expressions. Without anger or harm, help those who need to relearn and remember what love is. That is what our mission is here with you. This is how we will all go forward together. A new world of freedom is upon us all, and we are capable of the responsibility this requires through the acceptance and practice of Love. We are calling to you. All of us, plants and animals, are calling to you, "Wake up! Wake up now! Time to come home!" As our "relatives" the Borg have said, "Resistance is futile!" There is no need to resist. Love does not require it. Beauty does not require it. Life does not require it. Let us kiss your faces as we do the flowers. All is well. Love each other. It isn't hard. Accept each other. It isn't hard. Look to the life all around you for support. We are here for you. We yearn for the glorious colors you throw when you live in your true light. No more boxes, no more suits. Glorious colors all around like exquisite flowers in the garden of Happiness. It is the truth. It is you.

Mary: "Thank you sooooo much for your words."

Bees: "No problem."

Queen: "Come again in spirit to us. We are friends, and we value your time with us. Send us love, for we are entering the season of our hardship, and love sustains us. Come again. *All* of you. Come again."

The Song of Bees

I did not know
that I needed the song of bees
to let me know what my inner life sounds like.

I did not know
that I needed dirt
and water
and the smell of mulch
to remind me how lucky I am
to feel the sun,
to touch the grass,
to feel the rhythm of the day.

I did not know
I needed to hear the song of bees
as background music to my mind
or that their music keeps things in simple order.

—Renata Reid
January 28, 2014

Six

CHILDREN IN THE GARDEN

Why try to explain
miracles to your kids
when you can just
have them plant
a garden?

—Robert Brault

As a child, I didn't do a lot of gardening, but I always loved the flowers that my mom grew. I would pick vases full of fragrant gardenias and bright red amaryllis, and I especially loved eating the flavorful, fuzzy centers of her garden hibiscus. I was delighted when she set up little gardening plots for each of us. From the tiny zinnia seeds I planted grew tall plants full of happy flowers. My mom planted the seeds of gardening within my heart, and they've blossomed into a lifelong passion of love.

When you garden with children, it often has a profound effect on their lives and yours—it's an experience that can last a lifetime. Through gardening, children have the opportunity to touch nature in an intimate way. They place their hands in the dirt and marvel at the tiny seeds that they know will grow and bloom and bear fruit. They learn to nourish those seeds with water and with love and then witness the joy of birth as the seeds sprout and the tiny seedlings emerge from the ground. They learn the importance of commitment as they tend to their plants daily, and they enjoy picking the fruits of their labors when it's harvest time—their reward for a job well done. The most beneficial garden experience you can offer a child is to create a garden that follows organic principles and is inclusive—meaning all are welcome in the garden—so that she learns to work with the birds and insects, not against them. This will teach a child to respect Nature, as they observe the interconnectedness of all forms of life in the garden. There can be disappointments along the way, especially when tender seedlings are eaten, either by birds or insects, or when mature plants are compromised by wind, heat, or cold. You can help the child to understand that this can happen in any garden from time to time and that there are no enemies in nature. You can discuss solutions, such as placing little plastic sleeves around tender seedlings to protect them. (Plastic drinking cups with the bottom cut out will work well for this.) This keeps the seedlings warm and protected from the wind, and it protects them from nibbling critters too. Another solution is to create protective barriers, such as wind structures, which defend the tender seedlings and mature plants against harsh weather conditions, particularly strong winds. Creating peaceful solutions in the garden will teach a child to create peaceful solutions when they encounter other conflicts in their lives. If the birds and insects as well as the environmental conditions (wind and such) are not seen as enemies, a child learns acceptance of what is and how best to work with it. What a beautiful teaching model for how to move through the world! It's all about choosing love, and often children will embrace this way of life unless they're taught otherwise. The child who is given the opportunity to place his or her hands in the soil (instead of being afraid that the dirt carries germs) and is encouraged to explore the world of insects that live in the soil (instead of killing them because they're taught that bugs are bad) is a child who benefits greatly from this loving connection to the Earth. He will likely grow up to make better life decisions because he knows the value of our Mother Earth. After all, he's touched her with his eyes, hands, and heart.

Another wonderful benefit from gardening with children is the learning they receive from growing their own food. From seed to plant to blossom, they watch as the cycle unfolds. They learn about the pollinators that come to visit as well as all the other critters that call the garden their home. They watch the fruit develop and slowly ripen on the vine, and when it's harvest time, they'll gleefully pick their prize. With juice dripping down their chins, they delight in the first taste of homegrown freshness, grown from the seeds they planted and the plants they've nurtured all through the season. Life will never be the same!

Through my years of gardening, I've shared such fun with the kids that have come to play in the garden. I've included a few of those memories, plus some of the comments I've received from parents, teachers, and the kids themselves on what they love the best about the gardening experience. It's such a wonderful thing when you can see the garden—and all of Nature—through a child's eyes. Children in the garden—it's a beautiful thing indeed!

Every child is born
a naturalist.
Their eyes are, by nature,
open to the glories
of the stars,
the beauty of the flowers,
and the mystery of life.

—R. Search

SOME FUN GARDENING STORIES

I asked a few of my gardening friends and their kids what they like the best about gardening. There were lots of happy comments and bright smiles as they shared what they loved. It made me happy to hear all the funny, sweet things they had to say, and now I'll share some of that sweetness with you.

Brooke said that what she liked the best about gardening with children was watching her girls eat the tomatoes they grew. Actually, watching them eat all the wonderful organic food they harvested made her heart so happy! Her daughter Clare River said that what she liked the best in the garden was watching the flowers bloom. She also loved to water. Her sister, Charlotte Wren, said that she loved putting the seeds in the ground and watering them, and she loved seeing the kitty cats running around as she was putting the seeds in.

My friend Julie said that her favorite gardening experience happened when her young daughter Ally had just started to walk. One day she walked out the back door and made a beeline for the garden. Ally had her eye on a bright red tomato, and she grabbed that tomato off the vine and ate the whole thing. Julie said she'd never even eaten a tomato before and there she was, juice running down her cheeks and a smile on her face. Pure joy. What a great story! Meanwhile, Ally says that her favorite thing about gardening is that she loves to garden with her mom. That comment touched both our hearts.

Speaking of Julie and Ally, we shared a fun gardening experience at their home this past spring. Julie mentioned to me that when she walked Ally to preschool they would stop and admire an especially lovely flower garden on their way. Julie thought that Ally would love a flower garden of her own, so she asked me if I would be willing to help. Of course I was delighted, so off we went to pick out flowers, seeds, and soil amendments. We had Ally choose the plants and seeds that she liked, with only a bit of guidance from me.

She chose a new pair of gardening gloves and a children's shovel too. Her smile was bright as we loaded the flowers, tools, and seeds in the car, and off we went to create Ally's garden. We were planting in an existing planter box in front of the house that had previously been planted with bulbs and snapdragons. We dug them out first and carefully set them aside for replanting. The soil consisted of hard clumps, so Julie got out the pickax to break up the clumps and dig in the amendments. Once that was done, we helped Ally to choose the best location in the planter for each flowering plant. We worked together, digging holes, putting compost into each one, and then carefully placing each plant in its new home. We also replanted the bulbs and snapdragons, soaking the roots well to reduce the shock of transplanting. Next, it was time to plant the seeds, so we helped Ally to choose the best location for each packet of flowering seeds to be placed in the garden. It was so fun to watch her as she carefully and lovingly planted her seeds, watering them in with her little watering can. When we were done, Ally's garden was lovely, and it continued to shine all summer long.

I have another fun garden story. This one took place in my own garden as I was doing some late-season harvesting with my friends Scott and Elissa and their two boys, Tyler and Cameron. It was Thanksgiving weekend, a time when most of the leaves have dropped from the trees and the garden has gone to sleep. The runner beans that were full of beautiful flowers all summer long were now shriveled and brown, but their long bean pods were still hanging as they dried on the vine. Usually by late fall they're ready to harvest, and this year we had help. Steve and I grow a variety of runner beans, as we love the different-colored flowers (red, peach, white, and lavender), and you never know which beans you'll find when you break open a pod. It was so much fun to watch the boys—and mom and dad too—as they gleefully opened pods to find their prize inside. Brightly colored beans tumbled into open hands in shades of white, purple, black, brown, and everything in between. The beans cross-pollinate, so at season's end, we're blessed with an array of colors you won't find in a seed packet, which is a really cool thing! We spent a happy hour or more in the garden picking beans. It was like a treasure hunt for the boys (and dad too), and all were grinning from ear to ear. Eventually we all had to stop and head inside, as our hands were getting too cold to pick any longer (it was late November, after all). The family left for home to shuck the rest of their beans, and I did the same. It seems that whenever children visit the garden, it gets filled with such joy that I find myself smiling for hours after their visit. That day was especially fun for me, and I remember smiling for a long time. And now, when I think back on it, I find that I'm smiling still.

I asked Elissa if she could share some of her insights on gardening with children and also some of her experiences with healthy eating habits for kids. She had some good information to share, so thank you, Elissa.

As the parent of two young boys, ages five and three, I am constantly trying to find ways to trick, coerce, bargain, and bribe them into eating their vegetables and trying new foods. Tyler, my five-year-old, is inherently picky, often sensitive (to the point of gagging) to new smells, tastes, and textures. Cameron, my three-year-old, isn't really picky. He just copies whatever his big brother does. I have tried with some success mixing vegetables into smoothies, baking with vegetable purees, and making them sit at the dinner table until they try new foods. But the most successful trick I have found is making the boys a part of the process.

On a day-to-day basis, I try to have them help me pick out foods at the grocery store, help me prepare or cook those foods, and bake with them. They are decidedly more willing to try something if they have a vested interest in how it was made and prepared. To take it a step further, in the summer months, I have a small vegetable garden. I also have an apple tree and berry bushes. Because we live at seven thousand feet in the mountains, our growing season is short. Even in the summer months, the nights are cold. This inherently limits the types of produce I can grow. I stick to strawberries, beans, lettuce, broccoli, and small peppers. But the payoff of growing these foods with the boys is an invaluable experience for them.

We are so detached from our foods. We think produce just appears in our grocery stores. To have my boys put their hands in the Earth, plant seeds, nurture seedlings, feed and water them, and finally harvest the fruits of the labors is an invaluable lesson for them. I just love to water them, go outside and run to the garden to see if any strawberries have ripened, or pick an apple off the tree and eat it right then and there. Harvesting and shucking beans is another favorite. And you know what? They will try any new food that they have helped grow.

I have also been a K–12 special education teacher for the last twelve years, focusing on children with mild to moderate disabilities. I see kids with learning disabilities, autism, ADHD, and any number of other medical conditions and disabilities. When I first began my teaching career, I worked for Los Angeles Unified School District at a middle school. I was appalled that although these students lived only ten miles from the beach, more than half had never seen the waves or felt the sand on their feet. Although we live in southern California, a huge producer of citrus and other agriculture, most had never been to a farm, grove, or orchard. These students knew abstractly that food is grown and raised on farms, but very few had any real, experiential knowledge. Part of this is a socioeconomic divide. Students whose families have some money tend to be more worldly; they see and do more than those who are struggling to pay rent and have food on the table. My students not only had limited world experiences but also had, as a whole, atrocious diets.

I have since moved to the San Bernardino Mountains, where I have taught for the last nine years, and the students' diets are equally deplorable. Yes, we still teach the food pyramid. And no, donuts, chips, cookies, and soda are still not part of it. Every so often, I have a parent who puts forth a concerted effort to clean up his or her child's diet in a last-ditch attempt to alleviate the child's disability. Usually, the parent has read about going gluten free for a child with autism or regulating sugar and caffeine for a child with ADHD. Cleaning up one's diet works. It may not make the disability go away, but it improves the symptoms. My claims are just based on my observations and experiences as a teacher with an MA and twelve years of experience teaching hundreds of students with disabilities. I have seen it time and time again—when the diet is cleaned up, symptoms of disabilities improve. Attention improves, hyperactivity lessens, and sleep patterns regulate.

Sadly, the cheapest foods on the market are the unhealthiest. White bread is cheaper than whole-grain or sprouted bread. Juice drinks made with refined sugar are cheaper than fruit juice. Fresh fruits and vegetables are expensive. And to a family who needs to pinch pennies? Forget buying anything organic. Sometimes parents do what they have to just to keep food in their child's tummy. Schools are working to improve the nutritional content of the foods they serve. Some are adopting programs such as the Harvest of the Month, which brings fresh fruits and vegetables to the classrooms for students to try. But I encourage all parents, even those with limited income, to make the best choices they can. Avoid the soda, chips, and candy. Please. Your child will be a better student if they are given the proper food to fuel their little developing brains.

I want to share one last gardening story, this being one of my favorites.

I was living in San Diego, California, in the 1990s, and I had a friend whose young daughter attended a Waldorf school. I visited the school with her to see what it was all about, and I fell in love with it, so much so that I offered to volunteer there. I thought it would be fun to share my love for gardening (and the garden pollinators) with some of the students, so I offered to help them make a butterfly garden. They were so excited about the project, and once I gathered the materials we'd need (gloves, shovels, soil amendments, plant tags, flowering plants, and seeds), it was time to start creating our garden. First came weeding the plot and digging in the amendments. I found that each child was attracted to doing a different task in the garden, so those that loved to weed and dig were the first to get their hands in the dirt. The others helped as well but not as enthusiastically. Once the garden plot was weeded and amended, it was time for planting. We chose to plant the host plants first, those flowering plants known as passionflowers, which would feed the fuzzy black and orange caterpillars before they metamorphized into Gulf fritillary butterflies. The kids couldn't wait to see the caterpillars! Next, we planted the nectar plants, those flowering plants that would provide the food for the emerging butterflies. Each child dug a hole, gently placing their chosen plant into its new home and then "tucking it in" with dirt. We planted brightly colored pentas in shades of red, pink, and white; lavender-hued scabiosa; and the fragrant sky-blue flowers of rosemary, always a pollinator favorite. I also bought a few packets of flowering seeds for the garden. Brightly colored packets of zinnia and Echinacea were opened, and their seeds were poured into eagerly waiting hands. Each child placed their "seed babies" into shallow holes and blessed them with smiles as they covered them with soil. Once we'd placed all the name tags in their proper spots, the garden was done and we were *happy.* No sooner had we finished than the skies let loose and it started to pour. The heavens were blessing us, and with whoops and hollers we began to dance and splash in the quickly forming rain puddles. One of the teachers came out to check on us, and although he was usually a reserved guy, he couldn't resist whooping and splashing along with the rest of us. We all had so much fun! It was such a joyous way to celebrate our new garden, and from that rain-blessed beginning, it grew into a sweet sanctuary full of birds, butterflies, bees, and happy children who tended them all!

I'd like to close this chapter with a beautiful piece from my friend Deborah West:

I volunteer with children from broken homes. I do art, storytelling, drama, and kids' events. I get them exploring Nature through going to the ocean, going on hikes to see the amazing banyan trees we need to save from development, and taking them to lakes to feed fish, ducks, and turtles. I help them to notice beauty in flowers, sky, stars, and wind.

Seven

Our Animal Friends

Spirit of grace
and humor
on all fours.

—Pam Reinke

*I*t's morning in the garden, and I step outside to greet the day. I see my cat, Peanut, and next to him is a butterfly. It's a monarch on the ground, her wings fluttering in distress. I gently pick her up, and she rests in the palm of my hand. It's a warm day, so I know she isn't cold. I know Peanut hasn't hurt her; he was simply curious about her fluttering on the ground. I'm not sure what's going on with her.

She continues to rest in my hand as I do my morning chores. Even when I go inside the house, she doesn't move from my hand. I sit down for my morning meditation, and she and the cats join me. It's a rare treat to share a meditation with a butterfly!

I get a hunch that she has a message for me, so after my meditation, I grab pen and paper and we sit down to have a chat. She has much to share as she reminds me that I too am like a butterfly, transitioning into a brand-new life. She says I need to trust the process and be patient until it's time for me to fly. And when that time comes, I'll need to spread my wings and let go, allowing the winds of change to carry me into my next adventure.

I take her message to heart and say thank you, placing her on a bright orange Tithonia flower—a butterfly favorite. Just then, my friend Mary shows up, and I introduce her to my new butterfly friend. With that, the butterfly lifts off her flower perch and begins to fly in circles above our heads. She has more to say. She tells Mary that when I found her on the ground, she was tired and depressed and ready to give up on life. She has traveled far and wide, and the nectar-rich rabbitbrush that had sustained her on her travels was no longer blooming. There was nothing left for her to eat. But then she found the garden, where an open heart and open hand greeted her and a meditation revived her, and she was ready to live again. Even though it was the end of her natural life cycle and her days were numbered, she would spend her final days sipping nectar and love in the magic garden.

So, who of us hasn't been touched by an animal? Whether it's a lick on the face by a dog, a gentle nudge by a cat, a happy squeal from a pig, the whinny of a horse, the chirping of a bird, the happy antics of a lizard, the smile of a dolphin, or the sweetness of a butterfly, we've felt the love and kinship we share with the animal world. Our lives are forever linked with theirs, and because of this, it's important to honor and respect them in all that we do that pertains to them. What does it mean to honor and respect the animals, and how can we make better life choices so their lives, and ours, are happy and healthy?

As in all things, it starts with us. As we begin to open our hearts and love ourselves more, the love we feel spills over into all areas of life, including our relationships with animals. We begin to question how we live our lives in relation to the animal world, and if we find that our choices have caused animal suffering, we choose again. If we eat meat, for instance, we choose animals that are raised humanely instead of being part of an abusive factory-farm system. If we eat eggs, we choose eggs that come from chickens that roam free instead of those that are confined to filthy cages their entire lives. If we use cosmetics, we choose products that are clean and cruelty free instead of those that are tested on animals. If we want a dog, we go to a shelter or find a responsible private owner instead of supporting the abusive puppy-mill process. If we go to the circus, we choose a venue that has amazing human performers instead of one with animals forced to perform under human domination. And when we want to experience the world of wild animals up close, we choose venues that are about rescue and rehabilitation or wild-animal parks that mimic the natural world of the animals inside instead of zoos in which a wild animal often spends an entire life in a cage.

These are just a few examples of how the choices we make mean better choices for the animals, and making better choices for the animals can often mean healthier life choices for us too. We're all connected, and it's a nicer world when the animals aren't just animals but instead we see them for who they truly are, our animal friends.

COMMUNICATING WITH ANIMALS

Most folks who share their home with companion animals often talk to their pets, but they don't expect to hear anything back in return. Many dismiss the idea, whereas others are open to the possibility but just don't know how to go about it. The way to communicate with animals is through the heart. It means connecting your heart to their heart, and the language of the heart is our intuition. It is a powerful form of communication. When we speak to animals through our hearts, they trust us, as the heart *always* tells the truth of who we are. The important thing is to fine tune our receivers so we can give and receive these heart messages with clarity.

A good place to start is to use the same connection techniques that were outlined in part 1 of this book. You close your eyes and quiet your mind, placing your hand on your heart (or focus there). Fill yourself with the love that you are. Once you feel the love in your own heart, you send it to the animal you want to communicate with. The animal does not have to be present for this connection to be made. Sit with this for a moment and feel the love that's being exchanged between your two hearts. Say hello to your animal friend and begin the conversation. Keep it simple. Ask simple questions, such as, "Are you happy?" You could also ask, "Do you like your food?" or "Are you comfortable where you sleep?" Use your intuition—the voice of your heart—to hear the answer. You might hear words, receive a picture in your mind's eye, or even get a feeling. Whatever way you receive the message is perfect. Some animals are shy, or they might not have a lot to say at the time, so if you don't receive a response you can recognize, just relax and keep sending them love. They will open up and either respond or not, but either way the heart connection has been made, and maybe they'll want to talk to you next time. If your animal friend does want to communicate with you, keep the conversation going until you feel complete. Don't make it too long at first, as you are still learning and honing your skills. It's better to keep your conversations short and simple, but practice often. You'll get better at it with time.

To improve your communication skills, you could also take a class from a qualified animal communicator, such as those classes offered by Marta Williams, Carol Gurney, or Penelope Smith. I've been told these classes are fun and informative, and these women also offer books on animal communication. You can find information about them, their classes, and their books on their websites.

SOME ANIMAL STORIES

Through my own communication process with the animals, I've discovered they are quite aware of the world around them and not just of their own lives. Often, my cats know when my life is stressful or when I'm sad or grieving about something or someone. They seem to be especially attuned to my grief and become extra attentive and snuggly when they sense my deep sadness. They always know.

Animals are also in tune with their own and each other's grief. This past summer, we had to let our dear Kali-Kitty go. After returning from the vet's office, we laid her down by our fig tree. Steve had wrapped her in her favorite blue blankie (as he called it), and Peanut came over to investigate. He sniffed the blanket and then snuggled in right next to her and remained there until it was time to bury her. He was saying good-bye.

Another way that animals are attentive to each other is when things happen that are out of their routine, such as when one of them has to go the vet, for instance. When we got our only female cat, Samantha, spayed, I returned from the vet's office and all the cats were on the porch waiting for her return. I set the carrier down and opened the door, and she stepped out. Each cat went up to her and touched noses and then sniffed and licked her. They were welcoming their princess home again.

One of the many things I love about animals is how gregarious they can be. I had a lovebird once, named Tooty-Frooty, and he was the friendliest bird I've ever met. He'd been hand raised, so he was imprinted on humans. He just loved everybody—the more the merrier. When I had parties, Tooty would go from shoulder to shoulder and just visit everyone until he got so tired he couldn't keep his eyes open anymore. I think all my friends came to my parties just to hang out with Tooty. I had a friend, Dale, who used to come over and take Tooty on "field trips." I'd come home and there would be a note on his cage that said, "I'm off with Dale shopping" or "I'm off with Dale to the movies." And, yes, he really did go the movies with Dale! He'd crawl down inside Dale's shirt and sleep through most of the movie, making an occasional chirp or two. That bird brought so much joy to all who knew him. He had the biggest heart in the smallest body. I still miss him.

I'm always impressed by the intelligence of animals; often they just amaze me. I used to have a dog named Red-Girl who was incredibly smart because she was part red wolf. One spring we were hiking in the Anza Borrego desert, east of San Diego, and it had been a very wet season in southern California. We were walking in a wash. It was dry, but there were signs that a river of water had recently run through the wash. It was a hot spring day, and Red-Girl was thirsty. I had water for her, but she decided to find her own. She stopped in the wash and started digging in the sand. I wasn't sure what she was up to, but she continued digging in the sand until, suddenly, she hit water. I couldn't believe it! She drank her fill and then nonchalantly walked on. How did she know to dig for water in the wash? How did she know the water was there, just below the surface? It still amazes me.

Even the animals that most people abhor are still full of spirit. Last summer, I had nightly visits and conversations with two cockroaches (yes folks, that's what I said—two cockroaches). I named them the goldies. They would come out every night at the same time in the same place, hanging out on the orchid table. Their antennae would be moving all around, feeling their world as they do. I'd say hi and tell them I was happy to see them. They responded to my friendliness, as it was a rare thing for their species to ever be greeted nicely by a human. They never left that room and seemed quite happy to find morsels of food (dead bugs, probably) around the plants. One day, later in the summer, only one goldie was there, and soon both were gone. I was sad. Later I found them all dried up in a big spider web, such was their fate. They died so a spider could live, and the cycle of life continued on.

There are some animals that can be especially personable, and lizards are one of them. (Fish are too, but we'll save that for another day!) My husband, Steve, used to have a lizard friend he named Taylor (after Taylor guitars), and every day when Steve sat on the porch, Taylor would come right up to him and start doing his "lizzie push-ups." Steve hung out with Taylor all season long, having conversations on the porch.

The last story I'll share is about how animals can heal and transform their lives just like we do. My friend's cat, Little, is a perfect example of this. Little was a feral kitty, and she was scared of everything. She hid in the closet most of the time, and I could never get near her. Eventually, Little opened up, and I could talk to her and pet her as she healed from her fears. Toward the end of her life, Little went blind, and that's when the true transformation occurred. When she lost her outer vision, her "heart vision" seemed to strengthen and she became a different cat. She learned to navigate around the house and in the yard, exploring more than she ever did when she was younger. She started to let other people get close, even letting them pet her. That was a miracle! Her last days were spent on the lounge chair basking in the sunshine, and she was so happy. She even let us pick her up and hold her close, which she would have never allowed before. Little opened to love, and it changed her completely. That little blind kitty was such an inspiration. Although she's no longer with us, her heart is with us still.

One of the big realizations I've had about animals is how they're evolving right along with the rest of us, as is all of Nature. This planetary shift of consciousness into a higher dimension of thought is affecting everything, including the animal world. Because the fifth-dimensional template is a world of nonviolence, we're all evolving toward that state. Even the animals, including the carnivores, are evolving. (Although it is my understanding that the more aggressive nature of some animals will not make this leap in consciousness and their species will no longer be represented on the Earth.) But I've been told that the cat family *will* eventually make this leap in consciousness and become nonviolent, as the cat body will slowly evolve into a state that doesn't require meat to exist. Yes, the lion will lay down with the lamb.

I've been experimenting with my own cat family on this issue. We've had many conversations about the concept of nonviolence, and I've asked them not to kill birds, lizards, and bugs in the garden—it is a sanctuary. These conversations have been met with various degrees of receptivity depending on which cat I'm talking to. Of course, at this time in their evolutionary state, they're still carnivores, so I feed them meat protein (cat food). They've been informed of the rules in the garden, however, and all four of them have done quite well. We are seeding the idea of nonviolence into cat consciousness. There are some folks who say that's just who cats are and what they do. Up to this point in their evolution, that has been true. But the world is changing. We're all evolving toward a more nonviolent state, and that includes the cat family.

There are some folks who want their cats to catch mice, especially if they're barn cats. That's the cat's job, they say. If the cats understand and agree with the job (and what cat wouldn't?) *and* refrain from killing other animals, such as birds, for instance, then the agreement works for everyone. Our own cats have killed a few birds in winters past, telling me they needed the extra nutrition provided by the "wild game." Our cats are more wild natured and still choose to sleep outside, and sometimes they've needed the extra boost during especially harsh winters. I've told them it's important that they eat what they catch—no torturing the animal by playing with it—and we've had success with that. It's a work in progress, but it's been well worth the effort. We've been especially firm about the cats refraining from killing any hummingbirds in the garden, and except for one incident when Peanut was still an adolescent, no hummingbirds have been killed by our cats. That's a blessing and a successful contract with the cats.

As you can see, there are many variables here. It's not a black-and-white issue, as each situation is different. Do the cats have a job to catch mice in the barn? Do they need the extra nutrition from time to time during the cold winter months? Are they still learning and evolving? My feeling is that it's important to remain open-minded and flexible in each situation. But it's also important to begin the conversation about nonviolence, and why not start with our own companion animals? Our cats are listening, and they've all changed and evolved to various degrees. The birds and other critters that live in my garden are certainly grateful for that.

While we're on the subject of nonviolence, I'd like to address the issue of eating meat. It can certainly be a point of contention between vegetarians and meat eaters, but what do the animals have to say about it? From the conversations I've had with animals and from the conversations that others have had with them too, it seems the animals are in agreement with providing us nourishment by giving us the gift of their lives. It is their service for us at this time. What they *are not* in agreement with is how they are often treated in the process. Animals are not livestock; they are living beings. They deserve to feel the sunshine on their face, the breeze on their back, and the Earth beneath their feet. That is life. We have strayed very far from this reality in the factory-farm system. The animals that gift us with their very lives are often terribly abused. They deserve to be loved and honored from their first breath to their last. They are not a commodity; they are our friends and companions on this journey. Many Indigenous cultures understood this concept from the beginning, but the "civilized" world has strayed far from the truth.

I'm a vegetarian because that's what feels good to me. I personally can't handle killing or eating animals, and I don't seem to need the kind of protein that meat provides. But there are many people who love it, and their bodies seem to need the grounding strength and nutrition that meat provides. My sister is one of them. Even though we are sisters, our bodies are very different. She has always liked meat and knows she needs it, whereas I've never been fond of it. It's a personal choice whether to eat meat, but whatever you choose, do it with compassion. If you eat meat and you raise the animals yourself, provide them with a healthy and loving environment. When it's time to kill them, do so with love and an attitude of reverence. If you don't raise them yourself, then *please* buy your meat as often as you can from a source that raised them responsibly. The key words here are free range, organic, and grass fed. And love, of course. Love is important. In this way, you are eating with compassion. The animals that are raised with compassion carry that in their flesh, their blood, and their bones, and when you eat them, that compassion becomes your flesh, your blood, and your bones as well. That's much better than eating animals who suffer from abuse. The abuse they feel becomes you, and that's not a good alternative.

Now, there are some types of meat that are produced *only* with abuse, veal being one of them. The calves are taken from their mothers at birth and live their entire short lives in a crate. They suffer from the day they are torn from their mothers to the day they die. The compassionate choice is to stop eating veal, because once it's no longer in demand, the supply will discontinue and the abuse will end. That's a good thing.

If you choose to hunt or fish, you can honor the animals (as is common among many indigenous cultures) by informing them of your intentions before you begin. You ask whether one of them would like to come forward and gift themselves to you, and then you stay open to what the day brings. If you are successful in your hunt or you have fish on your line, then you're grateful for their gift. If you come up empty-handed, you can still be grateful for the experience and try again another day.

As I mentioned earlier in this chapter, if you choose to eat eggs, it's important to purchase eggs that come from chickens that are fed organically and are free range. If you choose to raise them yourself, remember that your commitment to them is for life. After a certain time, the hens will stop laying, and unless you choose to kill them at that time (with blessings for their gifts), you'll need to provide a home for them for the rest of their lives, regardless of whether they're still productive. Again, they are not a commodity; they are living beings. I know of two women who just let their chickens go in the desert after they stopped laying. I was appalled. These beautiful birds who had gifted these women with so many eggs were just dumped off like trash. How can hearts be so cruel? They are family, as all animals are, and it's important to treat them as such.

The last point I want to make is that if people ate the amount of meat their bodies *really* needed instead of eating it at three meals a day every day, there wouldn't be the need for the factory-farm system. The consumption would be so much less. I know it's part of many cultures, but people can change. It takes a lot of energy and resources to raise animals—more so than to raise vegetables—so there would be less energy used, less waste created, and no more abuse.

In the end, we can all make loving choices and create a better world for everyone, including the animals. We are so lucky to share our lives with them, and every encounter is a blessing. Whether it's a message from a butterfly, a nuzzle from a dog or cat, a beautiful egg from a chicken, or a friendly chat with a lizard, it's such a gift to have them so close and it behooves us to treat them kindly. As I said at the beginning of this chapter, they're not just animals; they are our most precious animal friends.

Mas and the Turkeys
by Mary Tannheimer

I had a friend named Thomas (Mas) who lived a few miles from me at the base of the Eastern Sierra foothills in California. He was a saddlemaker, a shoemaker, and an all-around fix-it man. He lived with his family in a house that was a cut-up section of the Manzanar internment camp barracks. The house had been transported to his land by trailer and dragged into position across the property by ropes and 8 x 8 timbers. Every year the family had a big garden with corn, squash, tomatoes, and various greens, and they also raised two to three turkeys from chicks, which they slaughtered and ate for Thanksgiving and Christmas.

I visited Mas and his family throughout the years, and one season he had two turkey chicks—a brown boy and a red girl. I came and went as these two grew, and I watched them play with Mas, Alicia, and their children. They all ran together in the yard and played together in the house The two young turkeys flew up on the roof and ran around while the kids ran on the ground, "chasing" the birds on the roof. They all loved each other very much, and it was very enjoyable to watch them together.

Spring moved into summer, summer moved into fall, and Thanksgiving moved ever closer. I thought of this more and more as I would walk by the turkey pen and see the adolescents picking their food from their bowls and strolling around the pen near dark. The slaughter was approaching, and I couldn't see a happy ending there. I often stood just looking at the turkeys, wondering what this meant to them and how all this would come to pass.

My unsettledness continued until one day as I passed the pen, the red girl, who was the larger one, came right up to the gate, turned her head to look at me, and started boring a hole into me with her stare. *She's* really *got something to say*, I thought, so I stood quietly and listened.

She showed me many pictures of the life they had with Mas and said they were very happy here. Mas was a very good man, and they wanted to know him again when they returned into physical form, which would be a different time and place for each. They had known from the beginning that they would be killed and eaten, but that wasn't important. What *was* important was the *experience* of this life and what it would mean to each of them. They wanted to investigate human life from a close view but not be stuck here if it proved to be unpleasant, so being turkeys for Thanksgiving was experientially sufficient and, whether good or bad, would have a quick end. They were so pleased that everything had turned out so well and were both very happy to donate their physical bodies as food to this family that had given them so much joy.

Next I was shown a scenario in which two coyotes came running down the dirt drive from the street above, broke into the pen, and ripped the turkeys apart and ate parts of them. Blood and feathers were thrown everywhere, and growls and screams tore through the night air. The feelings of horror and despair from the turkeys were sharp, and they made it very clear that a death like this would be a thousand times worse than being killed for dinner and would make their deaths valueless. The red girl reiterated how much they loved Mas and how much they wanted to give themselves as food in return for all his kindness to them.

The last thing this girl said was that when the time came for them to be killed, she wanted to be last. She was more afraid of the killing than her brother, and having discussed it, he had agreed to go first, even though he had fears also. This way, she could watch the whole process and know what to expect, and death would be easier for her. I said I would tell Mas, and I knew he would agree.

Finally, the day came. I had told Mas what the turkeys had said a few days earlier, and he was quite sobered by it all. He agreed to their wishes. We smudged the area, ourselves, and the knife (which was more like an extremely sharp pick) and sang a Chumash song to honor the birds. I was told to hold each bird tightly because at the instant of death, each would begin flapping strongly due to an involuntary muscle reaction.

The brown boy was first, killed by a thrust of the pick through the palate and into the base of the brain. His eyes covered over, and he immediately died. I had a hard time holding on to him. It was as though his body wanted to fly strongly away with his spirit and not be left behind. The red girl watched it all.

As I picked her up to get ready, she looked at me, again boring in. I understood her courage and kindness and wisdom and felt the completeness of what was to happen. I also felt the smallness of the human conception of life and the circumscription of its meaning. I held her tight, the knife went in, and I felt her go. It was done. She never flapped, not once. She was perfectly still in her moment of death because she had understood its method and was no longer afraid. She stretched out, flew as spirit, and embraced it as herself, the truth of her life and ours.

We were silent awhile after. Then we cleaned ourselves with water and the smoke of sage. We buried the blood and blessed the ground with their feathers. We all felt the holiness of those moments and the connection between this world and the next. This is what life is—connection between all things, continuous and unerring in its completeness. This is what is real. This is the wisdom the turkeys gave to us that day, a most precious gift, far beyond appearances—a gift from the Infinite.

Eight

HONORING NATURE'S CYCLES

*To everything,
turn turn turn.
There is a season,
turn turn turn.
And a time to
every purpose
under heaven.*

—The Byrds

A ll of creation moves in cycles, whether we're speaking of galaxies or a honeybee hive. The healthiest garden will allow its plants and animals to unfold within their natural timing—to move through their cycles in tandem with the rest of Nature. When we impose our will on our gardens by using chemical fertilizers to green them up, for instance, we're disturbing their natural flow. We're feeding them plant steroids, and even though they might look healthy, they're stressed and unbalanced. When we grow our gardens organically, they're given the opportunity to absorb the natural elements they need from the soil, and they do so at their own pace. We might not win any awards for the first red tomato on the block—or maybe we will—but our plants will have strong roots growing into the Earth, and each leaf that unfurls and blossom that unfolds will be perfectly timed for that plant instead of being rushed by the false promises of chemicals. The same goes for insect life. Instead of grabbing a chemical pesticide—or even an organic alternative—at the first sight of a hole in a bean leaf, it's healthier to observe first and then act according to what is unfolding between plant and insect. Oftentimes, plants that are stressed are more susceptible to being munched, so make sure your plants are getting the nutrients they need. Is your soil balanced? Does it need amendments? Are the plants getting enough water? Or maybe too much water? Often you can boost the plant's strength and immune defenses with a foliar feed or soil drench using fish emulsion, liquid kelp, or compost tea. (Directions for how to do this can be found in chapter 3, "Soil Amendments 101.") Another thing to consider is the cycle of the insects. Each year, the weather patterns in your local area will favor the proliferation of some insect species, while other populations of insects might lessen. Is this a grasshopper year? An earwig year? A beetle year? Sometimes you just have to allow them to cycle through the season, making sure to keep your garden well nourished. Just relax and trust in the knowing that next season's garden will be different. This applies to the "beneficial insect" population as well. Some years might bring a proliferation of ladybugs, while other years might bring lacewings. Sit back and observe how it all plays out. Each season in the garden is unique, so trust that all of Nature is moving toward a state of balance. This includes the insects as well. Another consideration is how the insects cycle through a single gardening season. In our garden, for instance, the pill bugs and earwigs proliferate in spring and early summer. We foliar feed the target plants such as the runner beans to make them strong. So even though they still get munched while the insects are at the height of their cycle, the beans eventually recover and take over the entire garden. We just have to get the beans through what we call their ugly insect munched stage, and then they shine for the rest of the season. In some cases, there might be times when you need to intervene during an insect's cycle. When this happens, it's best to use organic methods, keep your touch as light as possible, and always act with love. I'll give you an example from our own garden. Each summer, at the height of the heat and dryness in July (we live in the high desert of California), the spider mites proliferate. Unfortunately, the combination of the intense summer heat and the effects of the spider mites have killed some susceptible plants in the past. Now, we watch for signs of spider-mite infestation and take action immediately. We use a spray of neem oil on the affected plants only, blessing the plants, the spider mites, and the entire garden with love. We use the neem oil in the evening after the bees have gone to bed. (Neem Oil sprayed directly on the bees is harmful, but ingesting it on the flowers is not). A few applications of the neem oil and we're done for that season. Other than that, we can usually allow the plant-insect relationship to unfold naturally without any interference from us. We just keep the soil rich and the plants healthy and hydrated, and we let Nature create the balance between the insects and the plants.

There are significant cycles that are important for the gardener to pay attention to when planning and planting the garden. These are the Equinox and Solstice cycles, the moon cycles from new to full, and the astrological signs that the moon passes through each month as it moves through its lunar phases. We'll begin our discussion with the Equinox and Solstice cycles, and then we'll delve into the importance of planting by the moon.

The Equinox and Solstice Cycles

The Equinox and Solstice cycles consist of four equally spaced days within a calendar year. The Spring and Fall Equinox are the two days of the year in which sunrise and sunset are twelve hours apart, giving equal hours to day and night. At Winter Solstice, we have the longest night of the year, while Summer Solstice brings us the longest day of the year. These are nature holidays, so to speak, when a strong surge of dynamic energy is released by Nature and the Sun.

At the time of the Fall Equinox, Nature has begun her new year, and the call goes out to activate the new cycle. In society, we are conditioned to see the new year as beginning January 1, but the true new year of the Earth begins three months prior to that date. There is an energetic shift that occurs at the time of the Fall Equinox, and we, as gardeners, can participate in that shift. How do we do that? First, we connect with all of our garden helpers: the plant devas, nature spirits, faeries, gnomes, and so on. Feeling the love in our hearts, we make the connection at the moment of the Fall Equinox. (Dates and times can be found in *Farmers' Almanac* or on an astrological calendar.) At that time, we state that we are here to honor the new cycle that has begun in the garden and that we wish to assist in its unfoldment. Even though it might seem strange to call in the pattern for the new year at a time when our gardens are still lush and full of growth, it's still Nature's new year. We can also call in our personal cycle, and, in doing so, we often experience a seamless transition from our present pattern into the new one we are calling forth. We can state our intentions for the new year and see how they play out through all the seasons. When we align with Nature's cycles in this way, it's amazing how much we can accomplish before the Fall Equinox rolls around again.

The Winter Solstice honors the delvic level in nature. The Devas are the architects that create the blueprints for all form. Just as the winter months symbolize a more inward time for us, so it is in Nature, with many trees and plants living in a dormant state, although their roots are still growing deep within the Earth. The blueprints for the coming season are being created by the Devas. They are hidden from us, just like tree roots are hidden in the soil. During this time of winter, especially at the Solstice, we can honor the garden Devas for their creations. We can also honor ourselves for all that we have created thus far in our personal cycles, and we can revel in the quietude of winter before we move into spring.

The Spring Equinox brings us the time of awakening and the celebration of the Nature Spirit Realm. There is a shift on the Earth at spring. The focus on planning, which is part of the Devic Realm, changes to a focus on action, which reflects the Nature Spirits. The months of spring bring fresh growth and a renewal of life. We honor the Nature Spirits for bringing the Devic ideas into form on the Earth as we embrace the beauty of spring. We can also take time to embrace our personal cycle as it continues to grow and blossom. Spring is a beautiful time on the Earth. It is one to be relished in all its splendor!

The final celebration in this cycle of Nature is found at the Summer Solstice. This is when the devic pattern has been successfully and fully brought into form by the Nature Spirits. Who doesn't love the richness of summer? It is a time of celebration on the Earth, a time of joy, laughter, and sunshine within all the realms of Nature. It's amazing to observe how the year has unfolded since the call was made for the new cycle at the Fall Equinox. The Summer Solstice completes this call—in the garden, and within our cycles—and it's a time to celebrate and enjoy all the fruits of our labors.

As the summer winds down and the sunlight softens, we circle back to the equal time of day and night at the Fall Equinox. Whereas a single note was sounded at the time we called in last year's cycle, now a full orchestra plays at the end. We honor Nature and ourselves for a job well done as we bless our gardens for their beauty and abundance. We thank our garden helpers for the magic they've created, and we thank our Mother Earth for another year of life well lived upon her surface. The circle (and last year's cycle) is complete, and, at the exact moment of the Fall Equinox, (or, at least, sometime that day) we join with Nature and call in the new cycle. And so it begins again.

PLANTING BY THE CYCLES AND PHASES OF THE MOON

The Earth and her Moon are deeply connected. There is a continuous physical interplay between them, and it is within this space that the dynamics of their relationship plays out. The tides of the oceans reflect the moon's influence, as do the tides of our own watery emotions. In the garden, the moon governs growth. Therefore it is advantageous to consider the moon cycles when planting the garden. First to consider are the moon phases. During the first and second quarters, we move from new moon to full moon. The moon is increasing in light, and it's known as the waxing moon. Following the full moon are the third and fourth quarters. This phase is known as the dark of the moon, or the waning moon. From new moon to full moon, there is an increase of light, and it's the time for new beginnings. From full moon to new moon there's a decrease of light, and it's time to bring affairs together or to a close. So, how does this relate to the garden? The first two quarters, which are about new beginnings, are the best time to plant, graft, or transplant annual plants and also to plant seeds. (An annual is a plant that completes its entire life cycle in one growing season.) The third quarter, following the full moon, is the best time for pruning and for planting perennials. (These are plants whose life cycle lasts for many years.) It's also a good time for planting bulbs, root crops, and biennials. (Biennials are plants whose life cycle is generally about two years. The first year they develop their roots and foliage, and the second year they flower and set seed.) The fourth quarter, which brings the cycle to a close, is best for working the soil, weeding, and harvesting.

Next to consider are the astrological signs. There are twelve signs in the zodiac wheel, and the moon passes through each of these signs every few days or so. Each sign is ruled by an element such as fire, Earth, air, or water. The three fire signs are Aries, Leo, and Sagittarius. The three Earth signs are Taurus, Virgo, and Capricorn. The three air signs are Aquarius, Gemini, and Libra. The three water signs are Cancer, Scorpio, and Pisces.

According to the science of astrology, each sign of the zodiac and its corresponding element has a certain "flavor" to it. In gardening, we can use these flavors (or attributes) to assist and support the various tasks we need to accomplish. The water signs are considered the most fertile signs, so when the moon passes through either Cancer, Scorpio, or Pisces, we have the best time for planting. The next best planting time is when the moon passes through Capricorn or Taurus (these are both Earth signs) or Libra (which is an air sign). Taurus and Capricorn will produce strong hardy plants, whereas Libra (which is ruled by Venus, the goddess and planet of beauty) encourages flowers to bloom. The least productive signs for planting are when the moon passes through Aries, Gemini, Leo, Virgo, Sagittarius, and Aquarius. At these times, It's best to do soil work and weeding.

The first day the moon is in a sign is better for planting than the second day, and the second day is better than the third day. Usually the moon is in a sign for two days only, so a third day is rare. The influence of each sign is greatly intensified when the sun and moon are in the same sign. (All of this information can be found in the *Farmers' Almanac* or on an astrological calendar.) When considering the best day to plant your spring garden, for instance, you need to choose the right moon phases—new moon to full moon. Then, within that two-week period, you look for the time when the moon is moving through one of the more fertile astrological signs for planting, such as Cancer, Pisces, or Taurus. You'll have a few options to choose from, and, provided it's a good day for planting weather-wise (not too cold, rainy, windy, or even snowy, depending on where you live), you can plant that day. If your chosen day turns out to be a bad weather day, you can choose again.

Sometimes our busy schedules limit us to only a few days when we're available to plant. In that case, choose the best day you can and specifically ask all your garden helpers for the extra resilience needed by your plants and seeds so they'll grow strong and healthy even if they weren't planted at the most opportune time.

Planting by the moon can lend an extra element of strength and balance to the garden, but it is only one factor, so try not to get too stressed about it. If you have the opportunity to plant during the best moon and astrological cycles, that's really great! If you can't, however, just give your plants the best growing environment you can, and let Nature do the rest.

As gardeners, it's important for us to honor all of Nature's cycles. We honor the seasons and the moon cycles, the insect cycles, and the cycles of plants. We allow the garden to unfold in its own time instead of pushing its growth with chemical fertilizers. We allow the Earth to teach us how to flow with life instead of fighting it. We learn to embrace whatever happens in the garden—and in our own lives as well—because we know that "there is a time to every purpose under heaven."

Nine

THE HARVEST

Earth is here
so kind,
that just tickle her
with a hoe
and she laughs
with a harvest.

—Douglas William Jerrold

I t's midsummer as I write this chapter, and the garden is in its glory; it's harvest time! The fruit trees have been gifting us with luscious fruit since early June, starting with baskets of bright-red cherries and golden-orange apricots. Next came the nectarines, dripping with nectar (there's a reason they call these beauties *nectarines*), and now it's fig and peach season. Our living room is filled with flats of ripening fruit, and the smell is divine. Out in the garden, fresh almonds are falling out of their fuzzy husks and onto the ground, assisted by the ever-present Steller's jays, who do take their share. Soon, the prune-plums and grapes will be sweet, ripe, and ready to pick. We're harvesting the second wave of lettuce, kale, and carrots (the first plantings were harvested in spring and early summer), and juicy tomatoes are ripening on the vine. The garlic and onions have been picked and hung up to dry, and the peppers are full of brightly colored fruit, ready for salad and sauté! Basil, dill, and other garden herbs are fresh and fragrant, along with our perennial herbs: rosemary, oregano, savory, and sage. We're not the only ones busy with the harvest this time of year. The garden is full of critters enjoying the bounty. There are hummingbirds, butterflies, bees, wasps, praying mantises, beetles, ants, frogs, lizards, finches, jays, skunks, and foxes that are all dining here too! The garden is inclusive, not exclusive, so everyone is welcome to partake in their own brand of harvest. This makes for a happy, healthy, and balanced garden for all to enjoy.

In this chapter, we'll discuss tips and tools for easier harvesting as well as methods that can be used for food preservation. We'll round out the chapter with some tasty recipes to give you some ideas on what to do with all that yummy food. Just being in the garden is reward enough, but when you get to harvest all its goodies, life gets even better! In the middle of winter, when you pull out a jar of summertime jam, you know you've arrived. The garden has come full circle, and you'll enjoy its bounty all winter long.

HARVEST TIME: TIPS AND TOOLS

Whether your garden is big or small, there are a few items that will make your harvesting easier. First, a good pair of garden clippers (or shears) is an essential part of the harvesting process. Also, get a pair or two of garden gloves and a lightweight kneeling pad, which makes life easier on your knees, especially if they're sensitive. A collection of picking baskets are wonderful, and you can usually find a variety of shapes and sizes at your local thrift store. For fruit-tree harvesting, a ladder or step stool is essential as well as baskets or buckets to put the fruit in. We use cardboard fruit flats for this purpose. (You can often find these at your local market.) Place the fruit, naval down, in the flats, and keep them in a cool place, out of direct sun. Remember to check the fruit daily, making sure that none are rotting. If so, remove the rotten fruit immediately and compost it. Once a piece is rotten, it will spread to its neighbors in the box, so check your fruit every day—it's worth it. You'll find that placing your fruit in these flats will allow them to ripen beautifully.

Once they've ripened, you can store them in the fridge, either to eat fresh or for future use, whether you dry, can, or freeze them.

Onions and garlic are usually ready for harvesting when the leaves start to fall over and turn yellow. Using a trowel, dig them up, being careful not to nick them with the trowel. Use a dry brush to clean off as much dirt as possible, and hang them somewhere to dry. We put nails up in our carport and tie string to the plant's leaves, hanging each onion or garlic bulb from a nail. Any place that is dry and out of direct sun will do just fine. After a few weeks, they should be cured and ready for eating.

We grow runner beans (pole beans) and use the beans dry (such as cannellini) instead of using them when they are fresh and green. We've found that the best method to cure the beans is to leave the drying pods on the plant through the fall. Eventually, the plant dies back with the first winter frost, and by that time the beans have dried and matured in their pods. We harvest them before the cold winter days really set in. We often spend winter nights shucking beans by the fire—it's a wonderful thing!

So, now that you have all this garden produce available, what do you do to preserve it for the future? You have a few options, depending on the type of produce and how you want to use it. The options are storing (root crops and so on), drying, freezing, or canning. I'll describe each of these and the tools you'll need for the process. It's so rewarding to have your garden produce available to eat through the winter and on into the next growing season. It's what gardening is all about and makes it so worthwhile.

DRYING FOOD

You have two options for drying food. One is to use an electric dehydrator. The other is to use a solar dryer. We use both at our house. The solar dryer can be used for the vegetable harvest, whereas the electric dehydrator is the best way to dry fruit. At first, we tried the solar dryer for fruit but found that the fruit spoiled before it had a chance to dry. Also, one of our evening visitors, a fox, had the idea that those chunks of food were laid out just for him or her. The electric dehydrator heats up the fruit quickly before it has a chance to spoil, and it protects the fruit from hungry critters. The solar dryer works perfectly for vegetables, as they don't have the sugar or the moisture content that fruit has, so they don't spoil as quickly. Steve designed a simple solar dryer, but you can buy them as well. He fashioned two simple wooden frames—like picture frames—and stretched a piece of screen across each frame. He connected the frames together with hinges on one side, so they open like a book. With this design, you place the food to dry on the bottom frame and close the lid. This protects the veggies from flies. They can be a nuisance, especially if you're making sun-dried tomatoes, which the flies seem to adore. The solar dryer is placed outside in a sunny location, and it's important to check the progress of the food daily as it dries. During the summer, it takes only a few days for drying—the veggies turn crisp and flavorful. You can bag them up in zipper-top plastic bags and store them in a cool place. We often store veggies in the freezer even though they've been dried, as they last even longer this way. Our favorites to dry are onions, squash, and tomatoes. The drying gives them a nice texture and sweetens them up, especially the tomatoes. Sun-dried tomatoes are a treat that shouldn't be missed, and they are so easy to include in your harvesting routine.

As far as electric dehydrators go, there are many models to choose from. They can have anywhere from two to ten trays, and they all have a motor at the base of the dehydrator that blows hot air through the trays inside. They have a temperature setting that allows you to adjust the temperature according to how quickly you want your produce to dry. If you are drying fruit, you slice the fruit thin—keeping the skins on—and place the fruit on the trays. Set the temperature high so the fruit dries quickly. It usually takes about eight hours for the fruit to dry. It should still contain enough moisture for easy snacking but be dry enough so it won't spoil. Just bag the fruit up in a Ziploc bag and place it in the refrigerator; you will enjoy its sweetness for months to come. If you have a bag sealer, you can secure your bags that way. If not, you can use the "sucking-straw method." With this method, you seal the Ziploc up, leaving just enough room at one end of the bag to place a straw through. With the straw, you suck all the air out of the bag, removing the straw quickly as the bag deflates. Then you close the remainder of the bag, sealing it tightly. The dried fruit should last for many months, especially if you keep the bags in the fridge. I especially love dried peaches, and it's always a sad day when they're gone. There's nothing like homegrown produce, that's for sure!

FREEZING FOOD

I've found that the freezing method is the easiest way to preserve your produce. The biggest challenge is finding enough freezer space for all your garden goodies. We have two small chest freezers, one dedicated to fruit and the other to vegetables, and we fill them to the top every year. All you need for freezing food are freezer bags and either a bag sealer or a straw (for the sucking-straw method). We freeze most of our vegetables whole, such as tomatoes, peppers, eggplants, and squash. (If the squash is big, we cut it up; if they're small, we just put them in a bag and seal them up—no need to skin or blanche them.) We usually shuck the corn, although you can freeze it whole. I prefer to chop the onions into small chunks, which is convenient when using them for cooking. I just open up the bag and pour some in. I like to freeze basil by stacking the individual leaves and placing them in a Ziploc bag. Another fun trick with basil is to make basil-tomato cubes. Using a Cuisinart food processor (or a blender), I blend up all the ingredients—basil, tomato, garlic, and a little olive oil—pour the mixture into ice-cube trays, and freeze them overnight. I remove the cubes and store them in Ziploc bags, ready to use for a scrumptious sauté! You can do the same thing with pesto—mix your ingredients (basil, olive oil, garlic, parmesan cheese, and pine nuts) and then freeze overnight in ice-cube trays. You'll have ready-made pesto all winter long.

Freezing fruit is a simple process. With peaches, nectarines, apricots, and plums, you just remove the pit and chop up the fruit, skin and all. Cherries are more labor intensive because the skin and the pit are so tightly bonded together. I use a cherry pitter, which makes the job easier, although it still takes time to remove the pit from each little cherry (but they're worth it). I remove grapes from their stems and bag them up. All berries are easy as pie—just freeze them as is. The same goes for figs; just freeze them whole. Frozen berries, grapes, cherries, and figs are like candy to me—I just love them! I use the frozen fruit for smoothies, but it can be used for baking too. Even with a freezer full of fruit, our supply barely makes it to the next fruit harvest; it's a precious commodity in this household. As far as thawing your fruits and vegetables goes, just thaw them enough so you can chop them. That's all that's needed. Of course, you can't use frozen produce for a vegetable or fruit salad, but using them for cooking, baking, and fruit smoothies is perfect, and they usually taste as good as fresh.

STORING FOOD

Those folks that grow root crops such as carrots, potatoes, onions, yams, garlic, and winter squash, have also developed various methods to store their produce. If you are fortunate enough to have a root cellar, that's the best way to go. Another choice for storage is in an unheated garage. Some folks also use whiskey barrels, old refrigerators, cabinets, and so on to store their winter hardy crops. Wherever it's cool, moist, and dark is best for storage. Whatever container you choose to use, especially if you store it outside, should have plenty of insulation, such as foam or straw, on the inside. You'll also need to insulate the vegetables with straw or sawdust. Sawdust is especially great for carrots. Remember to place them a few inches from the sides of their container for extra cold protection. If you wash your root crops, make sure they are fully dry before you store them. If your vegetables are stored well, they should keep through the winter months. Inspect them regularly to make sure you don't have any rotten vegetables or any that have sprouted. If so, remove them and remember to tuck the insulation back around the remaining vegetables. Do the same whenever you remove any vegetables to eat—having them well insulated is the key to your continuing winter harvest.

CANNING FOOD

There are two methods for canning, depending on the food you wish to preserve. I'll give you a brief description of each, and then you can consult a knowledgeable source in order to choose which method is best for you and how to do it. There are books, classes, and online tutorials that you can access and become a canning pro. The first technique is the water bath. It is ideal for high-acid foods. If you plan to can fruits, jellies, jams, fruit spreads, fruit juice, salsas, tomatoes, pickles, relishes, chutneys, sauces, vinegars, and condiments, then this is the method you need to use.

The other technique is called pressure canning. It's important to use this method when preserving low-acid vegetables, meats, poultry, and seafood. With these foods, safety is the key, and pressure canning heats the contents to 240°F, which eliminates the risk of food-borne bacteria. Even if you mix high-acid foods with low-acid foods, you must use the pressure-canning method.

On a personal note, we have an electric jam/jelly maker made by Fresh Tech that I just love. This allows me to forgo the laborious hand-stirring process, so I save a lot of time and effort in the kitchen. As long as you follow the directions, your jam or jelly will come out perfect every time. You need only to seal the jars, and the process is complete. You can use the water-bath method to seal them, or for short-term storage, you place the hot jam or jelly in the jars and the heat seals the lids enough so that refrigeration is all that's needed for a month or two.

In the next section, we'll learn how to create some tasty meals from all your garden produce. I've included recipes from my kitchen as well as favorites from family and friends. The best part of growing a garden is savoring its flavors, so enjoy this section. It's a lot of fun—and healthy too!

Garden-Fresh Recipes

*A seed hidden
in the heart of
an apple is an
orchard invisible.*

—*Welsh Proverb*

The recipe section of this book has been a lot of fun for me. It's a collection of some of my very favorite recipes as well as some wonderful ones from family and friends. Included in this collection are three traditional Russian recipes from my friend Ksenia, who lives in Siberia. I've gathered quite the eclectic mix of recipes, copied just as they've been written. Because of this, they don't always follow the uniform outline found in most recipe books. I much prefer the personal touch, such as those from Ksenia. Hers carry a Russian flavor in the way they're written, which adds to their appeal and authenticity. Plus, they're a super-yummy reflection of her country's cuisine, which I love, so I'm thrilled to include them in this book.

It will come as no surprise that I encourage all of you to choose local, organic ingredients when following these recipes. These include cooking oils, vinegars, soy sauce, maple syrup, cane sugar, baking flours, nuts, seeds, nut butters, and dried fruit. Also, look for nonirradiated herbs and spices, and choose baking powder that is aluminum free. When buying dairy products, look for those that come from organic farms, and purchase eggs that come from free-range chickens. Organic honey is important too, as the bees will be treated better. Buying local honey isn't always as good as you would think; often the beekeepers still practice factory farming with their bees, which is stressful for them. Organic honey ensures that the bees have been treated well. Choose your fruits, vegetables, and herbs wisely—organic and local, if possible. If you grow it yourself, that's as good as it gets! Another consideration for choosing organic is that you won't be supporting the corrupt GMO machine. Genetically modified foods (GMOs for short) aren't good for anything except lining the greedy pockets of a corporation that doesn't care about the Earth—only their profits. Who wants to support that, anyway? Stick with organic produce—it's better for you and for the Earth too. Last but not least, try to keep your carbon footprint as light as possible by purchasing local food. If it has to travel halfway around the globe to get to your table, you might try to find something closer. Fresh is always best, and it's tastier too!

So, with that said, just delve in and start making some yummy food. Your kitchen will be a happy place, and a happy kitchen makes a happy home. So, bon appétit, everyone, and enjoy!

Yummy Roasted Vegetable Pizza

Servings	2
Prep Time	25 minutes
Cook Time	7 minutes
Oven	350°F

Ingredients

2 cups broccoli florets
1 large red bell pepper, sliced 1" thick
1 large portabella mushroom, cut into ½" slices
1 tsp. garlic powder
1 tbsp. balsamic vinegar
1 tsp. spike seasoning
5 oz. baby spinach
2 tortillas or pita bread
½ cup pasta sauce
1–2 oz. grated mozzarella cheese

Instructions

Preheat oven to 350°F. Toss broccoli, bell pepper, and mushroom slices with garlic, balsamic vinegar, and spike seasoning. Roast seasoned vegetables on a cookie sheet for 30 minutes, turning occasionally and mounding to keep from drying out. Steam spinach until just wilted. Spread a thin layer of pasta sauce on each tortilla or pita bread, and distribute the roasted vegetables and spinach. Sprinkle with the mozzarella cheese. Bake for 7 minutes or until warm, checking occasionally to avoid browning the vegetables.

Pumpkin Risotto

Servings	4
Prep Time	10 minutes
Cook Time	30 minutes

Ingredients

2 cups vegetable broth
3 tbsp. olive oil
1 small onion, finely chopped
1 clove garlic, minced
1 cup jasmine or basmati rice
1 cup fresh pumpkin puree (or canned)
1 tsp. sea salt
⅛ tsp. nutmeg
black pepper to taste
½ tbsp. chopped fresh sage

Instructions

In a medium saucepan over medium-low heat, bring the broth to a gentle boil. Simmer while preparing the rest of the recipe.

Heat skillet over medium-high heat and add oil. Reduce the heat to medium and sauté onions until soft, about 3–4 minutes. Add garlic and let cook for 1 minute until fragrant. Stir in rice and 1 cup of hot broth and reduce heat so the mixture simmers. Stir often, cooking until most of the liquid is absorbed. Repeat with another cup of broth, and continue stirring until the rice is tender, about 20 minutes.

Stir in pumpkin, salt, and nutmeg. Season with pepper. Stir until mixture is hot. Top with sage and serve.

Vegetarian Stroganoff

Servings	4
Prep Time	10 minutes
Cook Time	20 minutes for noodles
	25 minutes for oven dish
Oven	350°F

Ingredients

1 package of elbow noodles or shells
1 medium onion, chopped
2 cloves garlic, minced
1 tbsp. basil
1 tbsp. oregano
2 tsp. olive oil
½ cup water
1 medium carrot, diced
1 zucchini, sliced thin
1 yellow crookneck squash, sliced thin
1 cup baby peas
4 tbsp. white miso
¼ cup sesame tahini

Instructions

Cook the noodles until they are al dente, drain, and set aside. In a large skillet, heat the oil and sauté the garlic and onion. Add the herbs, one at a time, and lightly sauté. Quickly add the carrot and stir. Add the remaining vegetables, stirring after each addition. Cook until soft. In a separate medium bowl, whisk the miso and tahini together while gradually adding the water until you have a smooth consistency. Preheat oven to 350°F In a large bowl, add the cooked noodles and vegetables and gently mix. Then add the miso-tahini mixture and gently mix together until well distributed throughout the noodles. Place the stroganoff in a large, oblong Pyrex dish and bake for 25 minutes. Serve immediately.

Roasted Potatoes with Rosemary

Servings	4
Cook Time	90 minutes
Oven	375°F

Ingredient

5 large Yukon Gold potatoes, quartered
2 cloves garlic, halved
1½ tsp. chopped fresh rosemary leaves
1 tsp. chopped fresh oregano leaves (or ¼ tsp dried)
sea salt and pepper to taste
2 tbsp. olive oil

Instructions

Preheat oven to 375°F. Place potatoes in a large baking dish or casserole. Add garlic, rosemary, and oregano, and season with salt and pepper. Drizzle olive oil over potatoes and toss to coat evenly. Bake, stirring occasionally until browned and cooked through, about 1½ hours. Serve immediately.

Renata's Squash Soup

Oven   350°F

Ingredients

2 butternut squash
½ cup raw cashews
3 large carrots, chopped and cooked in water until soft
1 medium onion
soy sauce to taste
⅛ tsp. nutmeg
4 tbsp. coconut or olive oil
4 cups vegetable stock

Instructions

Preheat the oven to 350°F and roast the squash. Cut the squash in half lengthwise and scoop out the seeds and string bits with a spoon. Place the squash in a cake pan face down, and fill the pan with ¼ cup water to prevent drying of the squash. Bake for 1 hour, testing it with a fork. It should be easy to penetrate. If there is still some resistance, bake for 10 more minutes and test again. Once the squash is done, remove from the oven and let it cool for at least 10–15 minutes before scooping out the flesh.

Take the raw cashews and grind into a rough flour. Then toast in a pan until brown. (Watch carefully so they don't burn.) Sauté the onions in the oil until they're caramelized. Blend all the ingredients together in a Blendtex or Vitamix. Remove from the blender and add to a large soup pot or crockpot. If you use a soup pot, simmer for at least an hour to blend the flavors. If you use a crockpot, cook for at least 2 to 3 hours.

Carrie's Vegetarian Stuffed Bell Peppers

Servings   4
Oven   350°F

Ingredients

4 red bell peppers
1 tbsp. olive oil
1 small onion, chopped
2 cloves garlic, minced
1 tsp. thyme
1 tsp. rosemary
½ tsp. pepper
1 tsp. salt
1 cup carrots, chopped
1 cup peas
1 tomato, diced
½ cup walnuts, chopped
1½ cups cooked brown rice
2 to 3 cups tomato sauce

Instructions

Cook the rice according to the directions and set aside. Preheat oven to 350°F. Wash and clean peppers. Cut off the tops and remove seeds and membrane. Steam the peppers for about 10 minutes, just enough for them to be pierced easily with a fork. Heat oil in a large skillet and add onion and garlic. Sauté for 1 minute. Add the herbs and carrots and cook for 5 to 10 minutes, stirring constantly until the carrots are soft. Reduce the heat and add the peas, salt, pepper, tomatoes, walnuts, brown rice, and tomato sauce. Cook for about 10 minutes until flavors are blended. Stuff the mixture into peppers, placing them in a casserole pan or dish. Stand the peppers upright and pour the remaining sauce over the tops of the peppers. Bake at 350°F for 30 minutes.

Stuffed Baked Potatoes

Servings   6
Oven   350°F

Ingredients

6 large baking potatoes or yams
3 medium scallions, minced
1 clove garlic, minced
¼ tsp. dill
1 tbsp. soy sauce
¼ cup broccoli florets
¼ cup grated carrots
1 tbsp. olive oil
¼ tsp. basil
⅛ tsp. curry powder
¼ stick butter, softened
¼ cup olive oil
¼ cup soymilk
¼ lb. grated cheese

Instructions

Preheat oven to 425°F (to bake potatoes). Wash the potatoes and place on a large baking sheet. Pierce each with a fork one or two times and bake for an hour or longer, until they're well cooked and tender. Remove from the oven and let them cool. In a large skillet, sauté the garlic and scallions in the olive oil and soy sauce until lightly browned. Add the florets and sauté for 2 minutes. Add the carrots and cook until they're tender. Now add the basil, dill, and curry, and mix well. Remove from the heat and reserve. Slice the potatoes in halves and gently scoop out the centers. In a large mixer, add the potato meats, ¼ stick softened butter, ¼ cup olive oil, and ¼ cup soymilk. Begin to mix at a low speed and gradually add the sautéed vegetables.

Continue to mix until all the ingredients are well distributed. Place the potatoes skins in a large, oblong baking dish, and fill each with the mixture, garnishing them with grated cheese. Reheat in the oven, 20 minutes at 350°F, until the cheese melts and the filling is heated thoroughly.

Carrot and Cashew Nut Loaf

Servings	One loaf
	Serves 6
Oven	350°F

Ingredients

1 medium onion
2 cloves garlic
1 tbsp. olive oil
2 cups cooked, mashed carrots
2 cups cashews, ground
1 cup whole-wheat bread crumbs
1 tbsp. sesame tahini
1½ tsp. caraway seeds
1 tsp. arrowroot powder
juice of ½ lemon
sea salt and pepper to taste

Instructions

Sauté the onion and garlic in olive oil until softened. Mix all the ingredients together in a big mixing bowl, including the sautéed onion and garlic. Add a small amount of water to desired texture. It should be similar to a quick-bread mix in which the mixture should be moist but not runny. Place the mix in a greased loaf pan and cover with foil. Bake 1 hour at 350°F. Remove the foil and bake for 10 more minutes. Remove from the oven, let it cool for about 10 minutes, and then serve immediately.

Veggie Rice Delight

Ingredients

2 cups organic short-grain brown rice
5 cups water
2 tomatoes, medium-sized, chopped
2 carrots, chopped
½ cup broccoli florets
1 medium onion, chopped
2 cloves garlic, minced
1 zucchini, chopped
4 leaves chard, ribbed and chopped
3 leaves kale, ribbed and chopped
2 banana peppers, chopped
3 tomatillos, chopped
3 tbsp. olive oil
1 tbsp. balsamic vinegar
1 tbsp. soy sauce
2 tsp. Garli Garni spice

Instructions

Place all the ingredients in a saucepan (starting with the rice) and bring to a boil. Make sure the lid is secure. As soon as it boils, turn the heat to low and let it simmer (don't open the lid) for 40–45 minutes until done. Once it's cooked, stir all the vegetables evenly through the rice and serve hot. This dish keeps well in the fridge, and you can freeze a portion for a future meal as well. You can use all types of vegetables and herbs, whatever is in season or available.

Oven-Roasted Herb Tomatoes

Servings   6
Oven   350°F

Ingredients

18 large plum or Roma tomatoes, halved lengthwise
½ cup olive oil
2 tbsp. each of chopped fresh parsley and basil
1 tbsp. each of chopped fresh rosemary and thyme
salt and pepper to taste

Instructions

Preheat oven to 350°F. Place tomatoes on rimmed baking sheet, cut side up. Brush with olive oil. Mix all the herbs and sprinkle onto the tomatoes half the herb mixture, with salt and pepper to taste. Bake for 1 hour and 15 minutes or until the edges are brown. Remove from the oven, sprinkle on the remaining herbs, and serve immediately.

Portabella Mushroom Salad with Red Chili Vinaigrette

Servings   4

Ingredients

6 tbsp. olive oil
20 oz. fresh portabella mushrooms, coarsely chopped
1 tbsp. chopped fresh cilantro
sea salt and pepper to taste
1 lb. broccoli florets
8 oz. goat cheese
½ cup roasted almonds, coarsely crushed

RED CHILI VINAIGRETTE
2 tbsp. Dijon mustard
1 tbsp. dark chili powder
¼ cup balsamic vinegar
½ cup olive oil
sea salt to taste

Instructions

To make the vinaigrette, whisk together mustard, chili powder, and vinegar. Slowly whisk in the olive oil until emulsified. Season to taste with sea salt and set aside.

Heat 3 tbsp. olive oil in a large sauté pan over high heat. Cook the mushrooms until completely softened. Add cilantro and season to taste with sea salt and pepper. Heat 3 tbsp. of olive oil in a small sauté pan over high heat. Cook broccoli florets until tender but not too tender. Toss with a few tbsp. of the vinaigrette and then salt and pepper to taste. Arrange ¼ of the mushrooms in the center of each plate with broccoli around them. Sprinkle goat cheese and crushed almonds on the rim of the plate. Drizzle with more vinaigrette. Serves 4.

Hearty Pasta-Portobello Bolognese

Servings   4

Ingredients

1 oz. dried mushrooms
2 cups water
2 tbsp. olive oil
3 tbsp. butter
4 portabella mushroom caps, diced
1 medium onion, chopped
1 small carrot, chopped
1 small rib celery, chopped
2 large garlic cloves, finely chopped
1 bay leaf
⅛ tsp nutmeg
sea salt and pepper to taste
2 tbsp. tomato paste
1 cup dry red wine
1¾ cups crushed tomatoes
1 cup unsweetened soy or almond milk
1 lb. fettuccine pasta, cooked and drained
⅛ cup chopped parsley (flat-leaf parsley)
½ cup grated parmesan-Romano cheese

Instructions

Cook the fettuccine pasta, drain, and set aside. Bring dried mushrooms and water to a boil. Reduce the heat to low and simmer for 10 minutes. Let them cool, and then drain the mushrooms, reserving the liquid. Chop them coarsely. In a heavy pot, heat oil and butter over medium heat. Add portabellas, onion, carrot, celery, garlic, bay leaf, and nutmeg. Cook, stirring occasionally, until tender, approximately 15 minutes. Season with salt and pepper.

Stir in the tomato paste, cook for 1 minute, and then stir in the wine and cook for 3 minutes. Stir in the tomatoes, reduce the heat, and then stir in the chopped mushrooms, reserved liquid, and milk. Simmer over low heat until thick, approximately 30 minutes. When done, toss the fettuccine with the sauce and top with parsley and cheese.

Split Pea Soup

Ingredients

2 cups dry green split peas
1 stalk celery, chopped
3 carrots, chopped
1 onion, chopped
4 cloves garlic, minced
¼ tsp. thyme
1 bay leaf
salt and pepper to taste
2 qt. water
2 vegetable bouillon cubes

Instructions

In a large soup pot, combine all the ingredients and boil for 20 minutes, stirring the pot every 5 minutes or so. Reduce the heat and simmer for 1 hour or more, until the peas are done. For a smooth pea-soup consistency, strain through a colander or mash with a potato masher.

Vegetable Barley Soup

Ingredients

3 bell peppers, chunked
3 onions, chunked
3 garlic cloves, diced
10 tomatoes, chopped
6 medium carrots, sliced
3 stalks celery, sliced
4 cups broccoli florets, chopped
2½ cups barley
2 tbsp. soy sauce
¼ tsp. each of basil, oregano, and marjoram
1 vegetable bouillon cube
salt and pepper to taste
1½ to 2 qt. or more water

Instructions

In a big soup pan, cook the barley, peppers, onions, garlic, and soy sauce for about ½ hour. Add the tomatoes, carrots, and herbs, and cook another ½ hour. Add the celery and broccoli, and cook for ½ hour more. Add more water as is needed during the cooking, and add more soy sauce and herbs as well as salt and pepper to taste.

Garden Pea Soup with Cashew Cream

Ingredients

4 cups frozen petite peas (or garden fresh if you have them)
1 cup celery
1½ cups onions
4 cups shredded lettuce
1 tbsp. olive oil
1 tbsp. honey
½ tsp each of thyme and basil
1 tbsp. miso paste
1 vegetable soup bouillon cube
2 tbsp. raw cashews
sea salt and pepper to taste
6 cups water

Instructions

In a large soup pot, sauté celery and onions. Add lettuce and braise for 2 minutes, stirring constantly. Add the 6 cups of water. Add honey, water, thyme, basil, and bouillon cube. Bring the soup to a boil and stir in the peas. Return to a boil and cover, and then turn the soup down to simmer, cooking until the peas are tender. Remove 1 cup of broth from the soup and place in a blender with the cashews. Blend on high until you have a thick, smooth cream. Set the mixture aside. When the soup is cooked, reserve about 1½ cups of vegetables and blend the rest until the soup is smooth. Add the reserved vegetables and pulse once or twice to slightly chop. Combine the blended soup and cashew cream, and serve immediately, garnishing with chopped parsley.

Tangy Hummus

Ingredients

3 cups cooked chickpeas (soak overnight and cook in a pan or Crock-Pot)
4 cloves garlic
10 tbsp. sesame tahini
2 lemons (squeeze lemon juice)
½ cup minced parsley
2 tbsp. soy sauce
⅛ tsp. curry powder
salt and pepper to taste
water to blend

Instructions

Blend the ingredients together, filling the blender about ½ full with water. Blend until smooth, adding more water if necessary. Serve warm.

Yeast Gravy

Ingredients

¼ cup soy sauce
¼ cup olive oil
1 medium onion, chopped
½ cup nutritional yeast flakes
½ cup brown rice flour
4 cups (or more) of water

Instructions

Blend all the ingredients together. Warm over the stove, stirring constantly. (A whisk works well for this.) Cook until the gravy thickens. You may need to add more rice flour if it is too runny or more water if it is too thick. Also, you might add more soy sauce or olive oil for flavor.

Mushroom Gravy

Ingredients

½ lb. mushrooms, chopped
1 tbsp. sesame oil
1½ cups water
1 tsp. curry powder
1 bunch scallions, minced
¼ cup sesame tahini
3 tbsp. white unbleached flour
3 tbsp. soy sauce

Instructions

In a skillet, heat the oil. Sauté the scallions and mushrooms. In a small bowl, mix the tahini and water. Pour over the mushrooms and scallions. Bring to a boil. Then lower to a simmer and add the flour with a whisk, stirring constantly. Add the curry. Simmer for about 5 minutes. You might need to add more water to get the proper consistency. Serve warm.

Fresh Pesto

Yields 1 cup

Ingredients

2 cups packed fresh basil leaves
2 cloves garlic
¼ cup pine nuts (or walnuts)
⅔ cup olive oil, divided
½ cup freshly grated parmesan cheese
sea salt and pepper to taste

Instructions

Combine the basil, garlic, and nuts in a food processor and pulse until coarsely chopped. And ½ cup of the oil and process until fully incorporated and smooth. Season with salt and pepper to taste. If using immediately, add all the remaining oil and pulse until smooth. Transfer the pesto to a large serving bowl and mix in the cheese. If freezing, transfer to an airtight container and drizzle remaining oil over the top. Freeze for up to 3 months. When you thaw the pesto, stir in the cheese before serving.

Nutritarian Parmesan (nondairy cheese alternative)

Ingredients

¼ cup walnuts
¼ cup nutritional yeast flakes

Instructions

Place the walnuts and nutritional yeast in a food processor and pulse until the texture of grated parmesan cheese is achieved.

Herb Dressing

Ingredients

2 cups olive oil
¾ cup balsamic vinegar
¾ cup water
¼ cup soy sauce
1 medium onion
1 garlic clove
1 tbsp. oregano
2 tbsp. basil
2 tsp. marjoram
1 tsp. cumin
½ bunch fresh parsley
2 tsp. sea salt
2 pinches cayenne pepper

Instructions

Blend well; taste for flavor, adding extra herbs or soy sauce if needed. Refrigerate.

Tofu Dressing

Ingredients

1 lb. tofu
1 cup olive oil
¼ cup fresh lemon juice
¼ cup soy sauce
2 tsp. sesame tahini
1 large onion
3 cloves garlic
sea salt to taste
1 cup (or more) water

Instructions

Blend well; if you need more flavor, add more soy sauce or tahini. Refrigerate.

Avocado Dressing

Ingredients

½ cup fresh lemon juice
½ cup olive oil
⅓ cup soy sauce
1 cup (or more) water
3 cloves garlic
1 tbsp. dill
1 tsp. cumin
¼ bunch fresh parsley
3 ripe avocados
sea salt to taste

Instructions

Blend slowly, adding avocados and water last. Be sure it's not too thick. The consistency may vary, so add more water if necessary. Adjust for taste, and add more herbs or soy sauce if needed. Refrigerate.

Lemon-Honey French Dressing

Ingredients

½ cup olive oil
¼ cup lemon juice
2 tbsp. honey
½ cup tomato sauce
½ tsp. celery seed
½ tsp. sea salt
1 small onion
½ tsp. paprika

Instructions

Blend well, adding water if needed. Adjust to taste, adding more salt, honey, or spices. Refrigerate.

Three Recipes from Russia
From Ksenia Chaika

Gruzinchiks, or Lazy Dumplings in Soup

Ingredients

¼ of a large head of cabbage
3 potatoes
1 small onion
2 carrots
1 cup flour
salt
seasoning to taste
parsley
bay leaf

Instructions

Fill a half pot of water and put on the stove. While the water is boiling, cut the cabbage. Clean the potatoes and cut them into large chunks. When the water boils, put in the cabbage. Add the potatoes 10 minutes later.

Grate carrots finely. Cut onions. Heat small amount of vegetable oil in pan and put in carrots and onions. Cook on low heat for 5 to 10 minutes.

DUMPLINGS

With the flour, water, and a little salt, take 1 cup of flour and add a little water and a pinch of salt to make the dough. Roll it out on the table, and in the middle of the dough, put the fried onion and carrot. Wrap the dough over the filling into a roll shape. Fasten the edges of the rolls and slice into equal pieces.

Add the dumplings into the soup along with the salt, pepper, and seasoning to taste. After 10 minutes, turn off the stove and add the bay leaf. The soup will be nourishing.

Gruzinchiks (dumplings) can be cooked as a separate dish, put into boiling water. I like it best as a platter.

Pickle

Take 7–8 tablespoons pearl barley, 2–3 potatoes (depending on the size), 4–5 pickled cucumbers, a couple of tablespoons of tomato paste, one onion, salt, pepper, bay leaf, and seasoning to taste.

Pour water into a pan, about half-full, and put it on the stove. Bring to a boil and add pearl barley. When barley is slightly undercooked, add the potatoes, which were cut into strips, and diced onions. Cut cucumbers into small cubes. After 10 minutes, add the other ingredients along with salt, pepper, and other seasonings. (I also add a bay leaf early on. They are not bitter; they have a pleasant aroma.) About 5 minutes before barley is done cooking, I add in a couple of tablespoons of tomato paste and pour in a little cucumber pickle from the jar.

When barley is done, I add a little greenery.

Russian national pickle is ready.

Vegetable Stew

Take one large squash (or a couple of small ones), a couple of carrots, 1 onion, a few cloves of garlic, a head of cabbage, 2 or 3 tomatoes, 2 or 3 peppers, 2 small eggplants, 2 or 3 teaspoons of tomato paste, salt, pepper, seasoning to taste, and herbs (dill, parsley, and basil).

Cut the cabbage and put it in a roasting pan or skillet. Simmer over medium heat in a small amount of water for 10–15 minutes. It is desirable that all the water boils away. For example, I don't like a lot of fluid in the stew since the vegetables themselves create juice during cooking. But you can add more water if you prefer. As soon as the cabbage softens up, cut carrots into small cubes and add to the cabbage along with some vegetable oil. I prefer sunflower oil. Cut the squash into cubes, put it into the pan, and then stir everything together. (I love to cut the vegetables into large pieces, as vegetables cut this way retain more vitamins.) Cut up the onion (I prefer cubes but some prefer onion rings), peppers, and eggplants. After 5–10 minutes cooking, add in the onions, peppers, and eggplants. (Do not neglect the onions, please, even if you don't like them in your food, because they gather all the smells.) Over the next 10 minutes, add the tomatoes and a couple teaspoons of tomato paste until all is tender. Add salt, pepper, and different kinds of spices, mixing in well. At the end of cooking, add the finely chopped garlic. When the dish is served, garnish with fresh herbs.

I hope you will like my recipes.

Heather's Favorite Fall Cookies

Ingredients

2¼ cups all-purpose flour
1 tsp. baking powder
½ tsp. baking soda
½ tsp. cinnamon
½ tsp. ground ginger
¼ tsp. ground nutmeg
⅛ tsp. allspice or cloves
1 cup butter, softened
1 cup organic cane sugar
2 eggs
16 oz. fresh cooked pumpkin, mashed
1 tsp. vanilla extract
12 oz. milk chocolate chips
1 cup chopped walnuts

Instructions

Preheat oven to 375°F. Mix dry ingredients and set aside. Cream butter and sugar until light and fluffy. Beat in eggs one at a time. Mix in pumpkin and vanilla until smooth. Add in flour mixture a little at a time until blended. Gradually add in chocolate chips and walnuts. Drop tablespoon-sized spoonfuls onto greased cookie sheets and bake 10–15 minutes (depending on oven) until golden. Cool on rack.

Apple Walnut Brown Betty

Ingredients

6 large apples, cored and sliced (about 2 lbs.)
1 tsp. cinnamon, divided
½ tsp. nutmeg
1 tsp. almond extract
½ cup organic cane sugar, divided
6 oz. unsweetened cranberry juice
2 tbsp. dried cranberries
¼ cup water
2 slices whole-grain bread
2 tbsp. chopped walnuts
¼ cup quick-cooking oats
2 tbsp. butter

Instructions

Preheat oven to 350°F. Combine apples, ½ of the cinnamon, ½ tsp. nutmeg, ¼ cup cane sugar, cranberries, cranberry juice, and water in a saucepan. Cook over medium-high heat until the fruit is softened but not mushy, about 10 minutes. Remove from heat and transfer to 9" pie plate or cobbler pan. Place bread in food processor and pulse to form coarse crumbs. Combine the crumbs, nuts, oats, butter, remaining sugar (¼ cup), and cinnamon (½ tsp.) in a bowl, working the mixture by hand to blend. Sprinkle over apples and bake uncovered 20–25 minutes until lightly browned. Serves 6.

Tofu Mango Nut Pudding

Ingredients

1 package soft tofu
⅛ cup papaya juice
¼ tsp. vanilla
½ cup chopped walnuts
1 medium ripe mango
¼ cup maple syrup
¼ tsp. cinnamon
dash of fresh lemon juice to taste

Instructions

Place the tofu in a blender and blend on medium speed until creamy. Gradually add the papaya juice, fresh mango, maple syrup, and lemon juice. Blend well and add the cinnamon and vanilla. Blend well again and check for taste, adjusting accordingly for flavor. Pour into dessert dishes and garnish with chopped nuts. Chill in the refrigerator, and then serve.

Baked Apples

Ingredients

4 large baking apples, cleaned and cored
½ cup sesame tahini
½ cup raisins
½ cup chopped walnuts
3 tbsp. maple syrup
1 tbsp. cinnamon
½ cup water

Instructions

Preheat oven to 375°F. In a shallow baking dish, add the water. In a bowl, mix the tahini, raisins, nuts, maple syrup, and cinnamon. Drizzle the tahini mixture into each apple. Place the apples in the baking dish and bake until soft and tender, approximately 35 minutes. Serves 4.

Zucchini Muffins

Ingredients

1 cup honey
½ cup butter, softened
1 tsp. vanilla
1¾ cup pastry flour
1 tsp. baking soda
1 tsp. sea salt
1 tsp. baking powder
½ tsp. nutmeg
1½ tsp. cinnamon
1 cup granola, your choice
½ cup chopped almonds
2 cups grated zucchini

Instructions

Mix honey, butter, and vanilla. Set aside. Mix flour, baking soda, baking powder, sea salt, nutmeg, and cin-namon. Lightly mix the two mixtures together. Stir in the granola, chopped nuts, and zucchini. Fill muffin trays halfway with mixture. (Grease the muffin trays or use paper holders.) Bake at 350°F for 25 minutes. Makes 18 muffins.

Hippi Cookies

Ingredients

6 bananas, mashed
1 cup chopped nuts, almonds, walnuts, or cashews
⅔ cup safflower or coconut oil
2 cups chopped raisins
1 cup oat flour
1 tsp. baking soda
1 tsp. sea salt
2 tsp. vanilla
4 cups rolled oats

Instructions

In a big bowl, mix all the ingredients together. Drop spoonfuls on an ungreased cookie sheet. Bake at 350°F for 20–25 minutes.

Jo's Carrot Bread

Ingredients

2 cups soy flour
2 cups cornmeal
1 tsp. sea salt
2 cups grated carrots
1 tsp. baking powder
3 tsp. baking soda
2 tsp. cinnamon
½ tsp. nutmeg
3½ cups water
¾ cup honey
2 tbsp. yogurt

Instructions

In a big mixing bowl, mix the honey, water, and yogurt together and set aside. In another bowl, add all the dry ingredients together—the soy flour, cornmeal, baking powder, baking soda, cinnamon, and nutmeg. Slowly blend the dry ingredients into the wet ingredients, and then add the grated carrots. Place in 2 oiled loaf pans and bake at 375°F for 50–60 minutes.

Maple Pumpkin and Sweet Potato Pie with Easy Pie Crust

<u>Easy Pie Crust</u> (yields 2 pie crusts)

Ingredients

2½ cups whole-wheat or unbleached flour
1 tsp. salt
⅔ cup coconut oil
⅓ cup almond or soy milk

Instructions

Combine the oil with the flour and salt. Drizzle in the milk. Once you have the right consistency—moist but not too wet—pat into an oiled pie pan for a nice bottom crust.

PUMPKIN AND SWEET POTATO PIE

Ingredients

1 medium sweet potato
15 oz. fresh pumpkin puree
¾ cup organic cream
¼ cup organic cane sugar
2 large eggs
¼ cup pure maple syrup
½ tsp. cinnamon
pinch each of nutmeg and allspice
1 tsp. vanilla extract

Instructions

Preheat oven to 375°F. To make your pumpkin puree, first cut the small pumpkin in half and scoop out the seeds. Place the pumpkin halves (face up) and the sweet potato on a baking sheet lined with foil. Roast for 40–45 minutes until they're soft and easy to puree. Once they're cool enough to handle, scoop the pumpkin meat out of its skin and blend well until it's smooth, like pudding. Measure out 15 oz. of pumpkin puree for the recipe. If you have any leftover, you can freeze it for the future. Next, take the sweet potato and peel and puree it in a food processor until smooth. In a large bowl, combine the pumpkin puree, sweet potato puree, cream, organic cane sugar, eggs, maple syrup, cinnamon, nutmeg, allspice, and vanilla. Mix well to combine. Transfer the pie mixture into a pie crust. To prevent overbrowning, cover edge of pie with foil. Bake for 35–40 minutes (sometimes longer) until the filling is set. Cool thoroughly on a rack (2 hrs.) before serving.

Serve with homemade whipped cream. Use heavy whipping cream, maple syrup, and a pinch of cinnamon. Blend together with a mixer until light and fluffy. Adjust the flavor with more maple syrup if you want it sweeter.

Ten

Love, Not Poison:
Shining the Light on Chemical Pesticides and GMOs

*Man did not weave
the web of life;
he is merely
a strand in it.
Whatever he does to the web,
he does to himself.*

—Chief Seattle

*T*his book is about love. It's about the love we have for the Earth and for our gardens and about the joy and beauty we feel as we play in those gardens. This chapter, however, is not about love or joy or beauty. It's about the other stuff, the stuff that vibrates at a much lower level, the stuff that includes chemical pesticides and GMOs. It stands to reason that once we understand the truth about how low their frequency is as well as how detrimental they can be for our bodies and our environment, we'll be led to make a different choice, a better choice. The choice will be for love, not poison, and it will lead us to a healthy body, a healthier planet, and a brighter future for us all.

What is a pesticide? It is any substance or mixture of substances intended for preventing, destroying, repelling, or mitigating of pests. Pesticides are used to kill fungi, bacteria, insects, and unwanted plants (that is, weeds). They work by ingestion or by touch, and death may occur immediately or over a long period of time. Insecticides and herbicides are both considered pesticides. Insecticides are used to specifically target and kill insects, whereas herbicides are used to kill unwanted plants. There are some herbicides that kill all the plants they touch, but others are designed to target one species.

By their very nature, chemical pesticides create a risk of harm to humans, animals, and the environment because they are designed to kill or otherwise adversely affect living organisms. Practically all chemical pesticides are poisons and pose long-term danger to the environment through their persistence in nature and in body tissue. Many pesticides are nonspecific and may kill numerous life forms.

This brings us to the subject of neonicotinoids, otherwise known as neonics. They are a class of neuroactive insecticides chemically similar to nicotine. The neonicotinoid family includes acetamiprid, clothianidin, imidacloprid, and thiamethoxam. They were introduced in the early 1990s by the Bayer Corporation as a replacement for older, more damaging chemicals, but there are scientists who claim they pose the same threat to nature as DDT posed to nature in the past. They are a systemic insecticide, meaning that they are absorbed into every cell in a plant, making all parts poisonous to insects. Their common mode of action is to affect the central nervous system of insects. They bind to receptors of the enzyme nicotinic acetylcholine, causing excitation of the nerves and leading to eventual paralysis and death. This specific neural pathway is more abundant in insects than in warm-blooded animals, so they are selectively more toxic to insects than to mammals.

This brings us to the subject of bees, particularly honeybees. Honeybees have a genetic vulnerability to neonics, because they have more of these receptors than other insects. These receptors provide more learning and memory genes for the honeybees' highly evolved system of social communication and organization. Unlike many insects that are able to detoxify harmful chemicals to a certain extent, honeybees possess fewer genes for detoxification. This poses a unique threat to the bees, and it adds to what is an already precarious life situation for them. First of all, if they're being raised commercially, their hives are transported all over the world through all kinds of weather just to meet our needs for crop pollination. Often, these crops consist of a single variety of blossom, found on a plant or tree, that needs to be pollinated by the bees. In the case of an almond orchard, for instance, the bees are transported to the orchard to pollinate the blossoms, which provide good food for the bees. But it's only one type of food, and a honeybee hive requires a variety of foods to stay healthy. Bees that are stressed, particularly during transport, are more susceptible to parasites and disease infection, so the hives are sprayed periodically with miticides, which can further weaken the bees. And then there's the practice of smoking the hive. Smoke is often used to pacify bees when collecting their honey, which is a form of animal cruelty. When honeybees sense smoke in the hive, they go into survival mode and start gorging on their honey stores in case they need to abandon the hive. This causes the abdomen to become enlarged, making it harder for them to sting. Is that any way to treat our precious pollinators? I think not. If all that abuse isn't enough, add the abundance of honeybee-killing neonics to their environment, and we have a recipe for disaster among commercially raised bees. Bee-colony collapse has become an epidemic worldwide in the beekeeping business, and it seems to me that the treatment of these commercially raised bees needs to change. We also need to think about the consequences of our own actions when we use neonics in our gardens or purchase plants that have been sprayed with them. Either way, we're poisoning the bees and the environment, and we need to ask ourselves if it's worth it. I don't think so.

Because of their persistence in crops and soil, sometimes for months or even years after a single application, as well as their concentrated presence in pollen and nectar, neonics pose a serious threat to bees and many other insect pollinators. Unfortunately, their use is becoming widespread. Globally, they are used on more than 140 crop varieties, such as cereals, cotton, legumes, potatoes, orchard fruits, rice, turf, vegetables, and ornamental nursery plants. Just like DDT before them, the use of all forms of neonicotinoids needs to be eliminated. In the meantime, you can make a difference by growing and shopping organically and by encouraging your local plant suppliers, such as nurseries and garden centers, to carry plants that are free of neonicotinoids. If you are interested in beekeeping, you can make a difference in the world by becoming a respectful beekeeper. Good beekeepers will provide their bees with a variety of organic wild forage, and they'll avoid smoking them when they need to access the hive. A good bee suit is all that is needed to avoid being accidentally stung. It's also respectful to take only the honey you need, making sure to leave the bees plenty of food for their own activities, especially before the winter season begins. Remember to thank them for their gifts. As you provide them a safe haven free of poisons, the bees will provide you with nourishing honey and the wonderful gift of pollination. It's a beautiful exchange, and it's what makes beekeeping so special, and in these times, so needed.

Next, I'll discuss the subject of herbicides. Herbicides (or weed killers) are a type of pesticide used to kill unwanted plants. There are selective herbicides that kill specific targets while leaving the desired crop relatively unharmed. Others, such as those used to clear waste ground, industrial sites, and railroad and railway embankments, are nonselective and kill all plant material with which they come into contact. Herbicides can act by inhibiting cell division, photosynthesis, or amino acid production or by mimicking natural plant hormones that regulate plant growth, thus causing deformities in new growth. Glyphosate (the active ingredient in Roundup) is a broad-spectrum systemic herbicide and crop desiccant. It is used to kill weeds, especially annual broadleaf weeds and grasses. It is now the most widely used herbicide in the US agricultural sector, with 180 to 185 million pounds applied annually, and the second-most widely used herbicide in the home and garden arena, with 5 to 8 million pounds used annually. That's a lot of poison!

An increasing number of crops have been genetically engineered to be tolerant of glyphosate. The first Roundup-Ready crop, created by Monsanto, was the Roundup-Ready soybean. Before planting their soybean crop, the farmers were instructed to apply a dose of Roundup to remove all other plants before planting. And once the crop was harvested, or just before, they applied a second dose to prepare the field for the next year's crop. The Roundup killed everything except for the genetically engineered soybeans, which created erosion issues. With this application schedule, hundreds of gallons of chemicals are introduced into the environment each year, which affects wildlife, insects, water quality, and air quality. Monsanto loves this perfect combo they've created, whereby farmers use their Roundup weed killer on their Roundup-Ready crops. It's a win-win situation for Monsanto and a lose-lose situation for everyone else.

Another disturbing use of glyphosate is with the growing of wheat. Standard recommended wheat-harvest protocol in the United States is to use glyphosate for preharvesting, which eliminates the swathing step. (Swathing is the culling of wheat, laying it in windows to dry.) This saves the farmer time, labor, and resources—all good things—but it's at the expense of the environment and the consumer, neither of whom benefits from the poisons being used. In March 2015, the World Health Organizations International Agency for Research on Cancer classified glyphosate as a probable carcinogenic in humans. I'm not surprised.

By 2014, there were twenty-three glyphosate-resistant weed species in eighteen countries. Resistance develops after a weed population has been subjected to intense selection pressure in the form of repeated use of a single herbicide. The result of this is that we now have superweeds. More superweeds means we use more poisons to eradicate them. It's a vicious cycle.

Another disturbing use of glyphosate has been to clear milkweed along roads and in fields. Recent studies indicate that this has contributed to an 81 percent decline in monarch butterfly populations, as the monarchs depend on milkweed to lay their eggs and host the emerging young. As you can see, glyphosate has nothing good to contribute to the overall health of the planet and is another chemical pesticide that needs to be done away with.

Next, we have atrazine; its use is quite prevalent in the United States, second only to glyphosate. It was banned in the European Union in 2004, as they found their groundwater levels of toxicity were exceeding the limits set by regulators. Syngenta (the maker of atrazine) could show them neither that this could be prevented nor that those high levels were safe. Atrazine is an herbicide of the triazine class, and it is used to stop pre- and postemergence of broadleaf and grassy weeds in crops such as sorghum, corn, and sugarcane. In the United States, its use exceeds 75 million pounds annually. According to the NRDC (National Resource Defense Council), the most recent data (2015) confirms that atrazine continues to contaminate watersheds and drinking water, particularly in the Midwest, where it is predominately used in corn production, and in the South, where it is used on lawn and golf courses. It is found more often than any other pesticide in US drinking water, according to tests conducted by the USDA.

Atrazine is an endocrine disruptor that can cause hormone imbalance in humans and animals. It is so potent that male frogs exposed to low levels can turn into female frogs producing perfectly viable eggs. This is alarming, as frogs are known as an indicator species, showing us the health of our environment. It seems to me that if a male frog becomes a female frog through exposure to atrazine, then we have a serious environmental threat. The use of atrazine, like all other chemical pesticides, needs to be ended.

The solution, again, is to go and grow organic—this way you'll avoid using or ingesting toxic pesticides. If you have a lawn, there are many good organic grass-food products you can choose from. Also, you might want to avoid too much contact with commercial lawns, which are often sprayed with pesticides. Purchase only organic wheat, corn, and soy products, and buy organic cane sugar. You also might want to educate others on the toxicity of both glyphosate and atrazine. If they do have pesticides in their garage, for instance, encourage them to take them to the local landfill when they have their household toxic-waste cleanup days. The more we embrace a life free of chemical pesticides, the healthier our lives will be.

Finally, let's take a look at GMOs. GMO stands for genetically modified organism. They are living organisms whose genetic material has been artificially manipulated in a laboratory through genetic engineering, or GE. This relatively new science creates unstable combinations of plant, animal, bacterial, and viral genes that do not occur in nature or through traditional crossbreeding methods. Virtually all commercial GMOs are engineered to withstand direct application of an herbicide, to produce an insecticide, or to do both. The interesting thing to note is that even though the biotech industry promises greatness in its food production, none of their GMO creations currently on the market offer drought tolerance, enhanced nutrition (just the opposite on that one), increased yields for the farmer, or any other benefit. In over sixty countries around the world, there are significant restrictions or outright bans on the production and sale of GMOs. These countries include Australia, Japan, and all of the countries in the European Union. Sadly, in the United States, where I live, Monsanto still holds much power, although its power won't last forever. As the planet continues to shift and the consciousness of her people continues to rise, the desire for these poisons will fall away and their production will come to an end.

Genetic engineering is completely different from the traditional breeding of animals, grafting of trees, or hybridizing of seeds. You cannot mate a tomato with a fish, but the GE scientists seem to be trying by breaching species barriers set up by nature. They are interfering with the Devic blueprints. The results are plants or animals with traits that would be impossible to obtain with natural processes such as crossbreeding or grafting. Through genetic engineering, it is now possible for plants to be engineered with genes taken from bacteria, viruses, insects, animals, or even humans. As an example of this, GE scientists took Arctic fish genes and added them to strawberries and tomatoes to make them more frost tolerant. That's dangerous science, if you ask me.

We must remember that living organisms have natural barriers to protect themselves against the introduction of DNA from a different species. This is part of the Devic blueprint. Because of these barriers, the genetic engineers have to use various methods to force the DNA from one organism into the DNA of another. The creation of GMOs begins with force, manipulation, and control. That is not healthy creating. Another thing to consider is that the transfer of new genes can disrupt the finely controlled network of DNA in an organism, which at any point can have side effects that are impossible to predict or control. The bottom line is that we're not working with the framework of the Devic patterns; therefore, GMOs are created outside the balance of nature. That makes for a very unstable creation.

In the United States, GMOs are in as much as 80 percent of conventional processed food. They may be hidden in ingredients such as amino acids, aspartame, ascorbic acid, sodium citrate, flavorings (natural and artificial), high-fructose corn syrup, hydrolyzed vegetable protein, lactic acid, maltodextrins, molasses, monosodium glutamate, sucrose, textured vegetable protein (TVP), xanthan gum, vitamins, and yeast products. At this time in the United States (2017), we still don't have the proper labeling laws we need to easily identify the presence of GMOs in our food supply. That's why it's best to look for the organic label as well as for the Non-GMO Project label. The Non-GMO Project is a nonprofit organization whose mission is to protect the non-GMO food supply and to give consumers an informed choice. They offer North America's only third-party verification for products produced according to rigorous best practices for GMO avoidance. Their thinking is that if people stop buying GMOs, companies will stop using them and farmers will stop growing them. Sounds like a good idea to me.

With the introduction of GMO crops, a serious nightmare has been created for many farmers across the United States. Because GMOs are a direct extension of chemical agriculture and are developed and sold by the world's largest chemical companies, the patents these biotech companies have on their products restrict their use. What this means is that the companies that make GMOs have the power to sue farmers whose non-GMO-crop fields are contaminated with GMOs, even if it is the result of inevitable drift from neighboring GMO-planted fields. Many farmers have suffered this injustice, although the tides have begun to turn in favor of the non-GMO farmer's rights. As I mentioned earlier, the new shifts on the planet will not tolerate such unjust behavior, and corporations like Monsanto will eventually be held accountable for their actions. Another example of injustice created at the hands of Monsanto occurred when they began selling seeds to farmers in India, promising them huge crop yields with their seeds. The poor, who were supposed to be made rich with these huge yields, actually found themselves deeper in poverty when the seeds did not perform as promised. Many indebted farmers committed suicide. This was a travesty created by the ugliness of a corporation who doesn't care.

Besides their negative environmental impact, GMOs aren't good for our bodies either. Because GMOs have been altered from their uses and blueprints, the human body doesn't know what to do with them. They are incompatible with its functions, and the body will attempt to flush them out as quickly as possible, which can be taxing on the elimination system, especially if GMO food is ingested on a regular basis. It's best to avoid them altogether if you can. The best way is to buy organic and to read labels carefully on all packaged goods. The high-risk groups for GMO crops include corn, canola, soy, sugar, beets, cotton, Hawaiian papayas, and summer squash (both zucchini and yellow squash). As a gardener, the best choice you can make is to buy organic seeds and plants and encourage others to do the same. It's up to each of us to make good food choices based in love, and eventually all the poisons will disappear from the planet. That will be something to celebrate.

Conversation with a Jug of Roundup in K-Mart
by Mary Tannheimer

I looked around awhile to find the gardening poisons and found them in a far corner of the store, which was good because I was much more inconspicuous there than if I were standing next to one of the main aisles. It is easier to talk without a bunch of people staring at me as I stand appearing to examine an object on a shelf while busily writing away on my yellow pad. Sometimes the manager of the store wants to know what I'm doing. Talking to Roundup would not go over so well.

"Found the poisons, OK…Roundup."

My first impression is anger. I see long, straight, pointed-end shafts jumping up and down at different vertical angles, vibrating ever so slightly. They are dark colored to black. There is something here that reminds me of chemtrails and also of plastic. Then, right in my face,

Voices (*angry*): "Who are *you*?"
    I go to the sunny place in myself, and they all shrink back.
Mary: "I am Mary, and I would like to tell your story as you see it."
Voices: "We don't have a *story*! We are all that is!" (They are aggressive, pushing each other. They have hopelessness deep inside.) "Humans have messed with us, and look what we have become!"

I see conveyor belts in a factory/plant, with nonstop constituent materials/bottles rolling by. It is a *very* large place. I hear:

"Depression turns to anger turns to violence," then:

"We are elements, just living our lives, and big machines come and scoop us away. There is lots of screaming as we are torn from ourselves and our loved ones. *Huge* machines trample our faces and smear us across the Earth mother. Our mother. *Your* mother. Why do you do this? Why do you hurt us? Why do you hurt *yourselves*? You form us into concoctions that are poison to you, in conflict with your very lives, yet you persist in your egregiously arrogant behaviors. Egomaniacs all! We only want to live our lives in peace! *Where* did you learn this?"

I begin feeling nauseous and like I might cry. I see large pits of dirt, probably mineral pits, being dug. They are already dug out a *lot*.

Voices: "We are happy with ourselves. Where did you learn to put us together in such a manner that we are competing so for our lives? Some of us can't be near each other, yet you force us to be so. It *hurts*! Doesn't it hurt you?"

Now I see chem labs with workers in white coats, lots of glass containers/beakers/flames, microscopes and slides, long hallways to glass rooms, people in Tyvek suits with hoods/booties, and so on, all involved in "concoctions."

Voices: "They are just doing their 'job.' They think they are helping. You cannot help the world if you are killing us, or anything else, for that matter. It is your fear that causes the problems you fight so hard against. What are you afraid of? We are not your enemies. We are your friends. We can help you. We only became violent and aggressive because of your growing fear over the ages. We can help you grow out of this and help ourselves too, but not if you kill us. You are a violent, disturbed species now, and you scare us mightily. It was not always this way and wasn't to have been this way. We have many healing gifts to give you if you would accept them (and us). Will you? We won't hurt you, although there are factions of us who no longer feel that way. Accept us. We can help you live a better life."

A K-Mart worker comes and moves things around on the shelf. I wait.
    I am now back to the labs; this set is a different one.
Voices: "They combine us in groups that don't get along well. We fight among ourselves for room inside our little enclosures." (Molecular chains?)
    I see long, drool-like shapes winding around like earthworms in the sun.

Mary: "Are these the black shafts I first saw, when they are first created?"
Voices: "Yes! What a shape for us! Mistake! *Mistake*!"

I feel a horrified sense of realization and betrayal.

Voices: "What have you *done*? *Stop it*! *Stop it*! What have *we* done? Powerless, given up our power!"

I see a particular "force field" around the Earth that was put here on purpose. It promotes and sustains powerlessness across the entire planet for *everything* on Earth. I hear nasty laughing in the background.

Mary: "OK, so what will we all do *now*?"

Voices: "Oh—that's a good question! Plastic is a *very* damaging creation for Earth. It needs to be undone. Stop making it (almost entirely). The workers need to be/become informed so they understand that prevention/cures come from inside the body/spirit. They are not imposed from without. Even prosthesis is possible—regeneration through the body's own processes. You do not have to be maimed or crippled, but to do this, your consciousness must grow and leave these concepts behind. Think of what that means in your life—to leave these concepts behind. Scary? Glorious? Impossible? Wondrous? You are at the controls of your life. It *is* possible to change *anything*. You don't like it? Change it. Don't be afraid. You *can* do it. You simply must want to do it with your *whole* heart. Back to plastic. You don't really need it. It is a false creation of convenience, made to generate money for particular interests and to damage the human body for particular interests. Step up to the plate and say, "*No*, I can live without you!" It will be inconvenient at first, but that's part of learning. Do you need all those plastic toys, bags, bottles, cups, cans, and shoes? It seems that two-thirds of your world is made of plastic—a *falsehood*. This implies that you are false. Did you think of that? Life is much more *real* than you let it be. How much falsehood do you live? Would you rather be real? We live at the molecular level, so we know how deep falsehood runs—almost to the core. That's *deep*. Do you want to be *that* false? We don't think so. It is helped along by your lack of internal inspection and the exteriorization of your lives. That is why our chemical aberrations are allowed. In those forms, we help you see your acceptance of falsehood. As you proceed to accept truth, our days are numbered. Hurry to accept it, for it helps everything. You are more than you think or allow yourselves to be. Look up and see the sun, the sky, the clouds. It's where you came from. Smile. Laugh. It's your true nature. Be kind, and kindness will seek you out. Retain your power—don't give it away to be used poorly, against yourselves. You can change everything by being your true selves, compassionate, strong, and loving. That's all it takes. Be your best at all times, and you change the world.

"Thanks for the chance to speak. Come again. We'll show you more. We know you now and welcome you into our world, existent, and potential."

Mary: "Thank you so much. You have been more than helpful. Something will come of this; I'm sure of it."

I found it interesting that, just two days before this conversation, I had been poisoned by inhaling plastic from burning paint fumes, resulting in my spending a complete day in bed with a migraine-level headache.

The information presented by the elements with whom I spoke was obviously personally relevant and therefore makes its importance undeniable through direct experience. Their anger is directly poisonous, no different than ours. We would all be better served by accepting Truth. Our health would be better served too.

GMO Wheat in 25 lb. Bag

January 29, 2017
Smart and Final

The store is virtually empty of customers, so I cruise the aisles looking at all the GMO foods and begin introducing myself.

Mary (looking at pastries, cookies, pies, and so on): "Wow, they've certainly dressed you all up fancy and colorful!"
Foods: "It's all fake! It's not real!" (There is much disconcerted outcry.)

Mary (in the cereal aisle): "Hello. I'm part of a book being written and would like your input."
Cereals: (No response; it's like they're dead, no feeling, nothing. Then, angry forms well up, like jinn, big, bulky, and angry, growling.) "We don't want you here—*go away!*"
Cereal boxes: "They control us. They're what's behind all this. It's what *they* want! We better not say anything!"

Back to dead silence and feeling.

Mary (in flour and grain aisle): "How are you?"
Bags (depressed): "Oh, oh, oh, oh."

Each type of milled grain has a different variation of depression.
    I decide to talk to a bag of wheat flour. The masa says, "It's all the same. You can talk to any one of us. The wheat flour is as good as any. He can speak for all of us. There are minor variations. Maybe we will butt in if we need to."
Mary: "OK. Thanks."

I imagine myself sticking my hands in an open bag of white flour and running my hands through the mix.

Flour: "Aaaahhhh. We love it when you touch us with feeling from your heart. We have lost our feeling. Even the worst baker or cook can give us great joy. We have to live vicariously. (I get images of a huge white factory room with stainless machinery.) We have no feeling left. It has been bred out of us. This is what you eat—the equivalent of nothing—when you eat us. There are little robots in here (inside the flour grains). They control what we do. (Do they mean nanotechnology?) We used to have control. We used to be your friend and help you live. Not anymore. (Factory noises—*loud*—in the background.) They have taken over our hearts and ground up our soul. (They sound very depressed.) Not much to live for now."

I think this must be why the cereal aisle is so dead…besides the jinn.

"Please touch us some more." (I touch the flour with my imagination.) "Aaahhh…so good. Alive. We want our lives back. We want to be alive. We used to be alive."

All of a sudden, a man pops in looking like a cartoon hero from the middle ages: leggings, tunic, pageboy hair, felt cap.

Mary: "Who are *you*?"
Man: "I'm the solution!"
Mary: "Well, what do you have to say?"
Man: "Please hold my hand. This is important. There is a vast reservoir of sadness here, and it is very old. Those behind this have forgotten their connection with the whole and are taking their anger over this out on everyone else except themselves. Common enough, eh? Don't confront the actual problem at its source. Kick everyone else around you, because you can. It's safer that way. Never have to look at yourself. Very safe, hmmmm. I come to you in this garb because we were still friends (wheat flour and humans) at that time. No monkey business then, at least not much; just straight interaction. Healthy and fulfilling. Then what happened? More and more anger, more and more pissed off, more and more jealousy, who's better than who—this is both on your world and off your world. This isn't just an earthly thing. GMOs were brought here. Just for you—to control you. Keep you sick. You're easier to control when you're sick. Can't control you when you're not. Sick in the body, sick in the head, all those little nanobots running around in there, crashing and

breaking things in the DNA. Your cells don't know what to do: 'What *are* these things? Ugh! Get them away!' Like nasty little horror creatures snickering away, 'Ha ha, ha ha, ha ha.' Angry, angry. Not very pleasant, is it? Why do you go along with this? It certainly is not in any of your best interests! They take your money and run—and your life, too, in the process."

Mary: "I'm having trouble staying in this conversation."

Man (and others): "This conversation is about death—your (humans') death if you keep this up. It's also being monitored, so the connection is being played with. Like the GMOs. Mess with the signal and the final product falls away. No life. No connection. Death. Early death. Notice how many people seem to be dying younger and younger? There's a reason. Poison air, poison water, poison food. You can't live without any of these things, and they're all *poisoned*!"

Mary: "Yes, they *are* all poisoned."

Man: "Carelessness, unconsciousness. Too much TV—buy this poison and you'll live happily ever after. Whaat? Come on, folks, get with it! Maybe you'll make it to fifty, maybe thirty. What's the difference? I can look at life through my virtual reality goggles and everything looks OK. Which program should I plug in today?"

A large voice comes in over the Man:

"Humans cannot continue this charade or there will be hell to pay. You are playing with your destiny as a species. *You* are becoming GMOs! Your lineage has been altered to fool you out of your heritage as creator beings in tune with the forces of benevolence in this universe. You can do anything, yet you think you are powerless—*so* powerless that you must rely on drugs and technology to stay alive after you've agreed to be poisoned by beings so jealous of your power that they have completely manipulated your reality so they can get some of that power. They can't make life, but they can destroy it. They have tricked you into living in a world of destruction so they can feed off your power without you realizing this is happening. It's the elixir of life for them—your *powerlessness*! It's not even *true*—how *ironic* that you allow this. Stop eating the poison. Stop watching the poison. Stop emulating the poison. When you do, you'll live a life full of purpose, *your* purpose, a strong fulfilling life, in tune with others, and you won't question, 'What is my purpose; what is life's purpose?' It is to *live* and be *all* you can. When everyone turns in this direction, you as a species will be unstoppable. The connection will be complete. Death will be no more. Manipulation will be no more. The Truth of your Being will prevail. Have faith in yourselves, each one of you. You each make a difference if you do your best. That is how you defeat ignorance and the lie of powerlessness. When you are in your power, there is no fear, no collusion, no treachery. It can't exist there. Your power stems from the One behind the creator, the Mind of Consciousness, where there is only Love. Only Love, nothing less. You can't fail here, so why not go? It's your future if you choose to have it be so. A poisoned world falls away and beauty and joy remains. Take off your VR goggles and see your true Self. You are beautiful. You are All That Is."

Mary: "I need to stop now. Very intense."
Man (laughing): "See you in your future!"
Pop! Then he's gone.

Mary (slight headache now): "Wow. That was a good one. (Sighs.) Guess I'll go home now and sit down awhile."
    I have run out of paper. "I need a new tablet too."

Eleven

GARDENING IN CLIMATE CHANGE

The goal in life
is living
in agreement
with nature.

—Zeno

These days, as gardeners, we're practicing what I call "adaptable gardening." In the northern hemisphere, the season may begin in early February, as we find ourselves outside in T-shirts and shorts, cleaning up the garden beds. Bees are buzzing in the crocuses and almond blossoms are shining with the first blush of spring. We're halfway through winter (otherwise known as Candlemas or Groundhog Day) and the sun is smiling a bit higher in the sky each day. There's a hint of new life in the air and we're all celebrating, as cats lie in the sun and gardeners tan their white winter legs. A week later, the spring door closes hard, with frost in the air and snow on the ground. The bees have retreated back to the hive, the crocuses are shut tight against the cold, and the beautiful almond blossoms have frozen and fallen to the ground. This thaw/freeze cycle may repeat itself many more times throughout the season, and we hope a few fruit blossoms will provide us with a harvest by summer's end.

After spring comes summer, with its own unique set of challenges in the garden. It's time to adjust to summer heat punctuated by intense downpours, strong winds, and occasional golf-ball-sized hail. The hail is the hardest on the garden, as tender veggies get pummeled and ripening fruit gets knocked out of trees. We love the summer season, especially the harvest, but it can be a tough one out in the garden these days.

Finally, we come to the gentle season of fall—unless, of course, it's hurricane season in your neck of the woods; then it's not so gentle! But many of us find ourselves in the midst of beautiful Indian-summer days and comfy autumn nights. We enjoy the cooler sun and bright skies, and we look forward to an abundant fall harvest. Usually it is good, but sometimes an early frosty storm can come barreling in, taking out our prize tomatoes, which die on the vine. Although gardening has always been a test of faith, it's even more so these days. Gardening in climate change means being open to these changes. As our gardens adapt and evolve, we need to adapt and evolve as well.

So, with that said, what does the scientific data tell us about the various climate extremes we're experiencing in the garden and on the planet? I'll give you some temperature records so you can see how this is playing out all over the world.

A joint report from the National Oceanic and Atmospheric Administration (NOAA) and NASA stated that 2016 was officially the warmest year on record, edging out the previous record holder, 2015, by .07°F. Through data collected from the two agencies, they showed that Earth's average temperature across global land and ocean surfaces was 58.69°F, or 1.69°F above the twentieth-century average. Since the start of the twenty-first century, the annual global temperature record has been broken five times, and sixteen of the seventeen warmest years on record have occurred since 2001. With 2016 being the third record in a row for highest global temperatures, the ongoing long-term warming trend is clear.

Besides the extremes in temperature, we now have extremes in the distribution of water as well. Some areas are plagued by intense drought, others by massive flooding. It may seem counterintuitive that both drought and downpours leading to intense flooding are increasing, but these are not mutually exclusive. Overall, variability in the climate has increased, which means that we are seeing more feast-or-famine swings rather than constant conditions. Because of the changes happening with our climate, many people have begun speaking of the greenhouse effect and the role the increase in greenhouse gases might be playing in a warming planet. We will have that discussion in a moment, but first it's important to understand what the greenhouse effect is, how it works, and why life on Earth would not be the same without it.

The greenhouse effect is a naturally occurring process that aids in heating the Earth's surface and its atmosphere. It begins with the sun, as its heat energy is absorbed by the Earth. The Earth heats up and starts radiating the long-wave energy (known as infrared radiation) into the atmosphere. Certain atmospheric gases, such as carbon dioxide, water vapor, and methane, absorb the energy and then direct over 90 percent of it back to the Earth. The Earth heats up further and directs it back into the atmosphere, and, again, as the gas molecules heat up, they radiate back to the Earth. This cycle will repeat over and over until no more long-wave energy is available for absorption. Without this greenhouse effect, life as we know it wouldn't exist. The average temperature of the Earth would be a chilly 4°F (−18°C) rather than a pleasant 59°F (15°C).

There is much speculation on whether the Earth is heating up, which it definitely is, and whether we're solely responsible for the increase in temperature, which we're not. The Earth and the sun share a complex and interconnected relationship, and there's more than one factor involved in the warming of our planet.

On one side of the fence, there are those folks who say we are responsible for our warming climate due to the burning of our fossil fuels, the burning of our rainforests, the manure emissions that come from raising livestock, and many other sources. These folks claim that the CO_2 has created the greenhouse effect and thus the rise in temperature.

On the other side of the fence, there are those folks who depend on climate-cycle records from the past. Their data shows that the recent changes in temperature are part of a well-established pattern and that we are living during a time when one cycle (a cycle of warming) is ending and the next cycle (a cycle of cooling) is beginning. Also, according to ice-core data, it has been shown that greenhouse gases—specifically CO_2—are not the cause of global warming, as the higher temperatures precede the increase in gas levels by anywhere from 400 to 10,000 years.

So, who's got it right? Did we cause global warming? Is the planet warming up or is it cooling down? Do our emissions contribute to this process? Is there a metaphysical aspect to all of this? And what role does the sun play in a changing climate?

Let me offer you an interesting perspective. It seems to me that the answer is really a blend of these factors and more. Gregg Braden, a well-renowned scientist and spiritual teacher, speaks of taking the best science of our time and marrying it to the wisdom of our past—our spiritual heritage—in order to gain a clear picture of our world. It's a blend of the two—science and spirituality—and it is the best way to view the truth about our changing climate.

The pollutants we spew into our atmosphere are affecting the atmosphere in unhealthy ways and contributing to its warming. At this time, we are locked into the use of fossil fuels, which extract the life-blood, the very lubrication, of the planet. This has led to pollution from emissions and oil spills, the detrimental effects of fracking (which leads to increased seismic activity), and pipelines often built through sacred, sensitive natural environments. The technology exists for developing cleaner, greener energy, but it has been repeatedly silenced and shut down by the greedy powers that be. This will change in the future as the greedy lose their power, but it will be a slow process. Meanwhile, we can support legislation that works to curb our emissions as well as push for the development of new technologies not dependent on oil. We can also lessen our meat consumption to the amount our body really needs, which will lessen the manure emissions from our farms, which is a good thing. With less consumption of meat products, there will be less produced and our abusive factory-farm system will be eliminated, which is an added bonus.

We also have to consider the ice-core data, which clearly shows the fact that higher temperatures *precede* the increase in gas levels. These ice-core samples were obtained in June 1999, as an international team of scientists completed a drilling project to the bottom of the thickest portions of ice—the Vostok, Antarctica, drill down. The layers of ice they sampled have given us a continuous window to 420,000 years into the past. The scientists were able to see precisely how the cycles of global temperatures and greenhouse gases play out. What they found is that changes in atmospheric CO_2 content never precede changes in air temperature. The lag time of the rise in CO_2 concentrations, with respect to temperature change, is on the order of 400 to 1,000 years during all three glacial-interglacial transitions. Therefore, the significant warm-up precedes the CO_2 emissions.

If that's the case, then what is causing global warming? My answer to you is the sun. The Earth is heating up from the inside out, as bursts of solar energy in the form of solar flares, solar winds, and coronal mass ejections (CMEs) are pouring onto the planet in huge waves. The Earth is lightening up, so to speak, and the sun is assisting in the process. Light is a powerful force, and the sun is playing a key role in the evolution of our planet through these bursts of solar light. Much cleansing and balancing is happening. These changes in consciousness are playing out on the world stage as we open our hearts to love and freedom and the unity of all people, while the powers that be continue to push for hatred and fear and the division of people. It's a huge event playing out between light and dark on the planet, and the light is winning, although you'd never know it listening to mainstream media.

The light will continue to pour onto the planet, and we'll experience intense times of weather-related cleansing and balancing as a partial result of the solar emissions. It will continue to be a wild ride. Therefore it's important for us to be adaptable and to be open to love most of all. Choose love over fear as often as you can. Love will lead us to make better environmental choices, contributing to our well-being and the well-being of the planet. Love will lead us to push for greener alternatives to our current oil-driven energy sources. Love will allow us to embrace the diversity of cultures instead of building walls of fear that separate us. Love will lead us to spend more time in the natural world to balance us. It's a fact that when we love something, we'll do all we can to protect it, so when we spend more time in nature, we'll do all we can to protect and care for the Earth.

It is my belief that we're in for some interesting times in the years to come, but it's nothing we can't handle. We won't starve, and there will be enough water for everyone, no matter what the doomsdayers say! We'll not only survive, but we'll thrive in the years ahead. It is a shifting time on the planet right now, not an ending time. Of that I am sure.

The Earth-Gaia and the Overlighting Devas are working together to bring about this shift on the planet. In tandem with the sun, they are helping to facilitate the weather conditions that are needed in any given area for the cleansing and balancing of that area. This is happening all over the planet, and it's not always easy. These patterns include heat, cold, dry, snow, ice, rain, wind, and the more intense weather phenomena, which include tornadoes, typhoons, and hurricanes. A huge planetary balancing is going on, and the weather is assisting in this. It's a changing planet, and the best things we can do are to be adaptable in how we live our lives and to reach out to others in need, especially during times of weather-related crisis. As in all things, it brings us back to love, and that's the best place to be.

Along with the cleansing and balancing that occurs with the various weather phenomena, there is also a heart-opening that happens at this time. People reach out to each other with open hands and hearts during times of fire, flood, ice storms, tornadoes, hurricanes, and even drought. The best in humanity comes out with shining colors, as neighbors help neighbors, communities set up shelters and clothing donation drop-off spots, fundraisers are held, GoFundMe sites are set up—anything that's needed. It's a wonderful thing to watch the outpouring of love that occurs at times of need. It's what makes us so beautiful! The shifting weather patterns and their corresponding weather extremes will be challenging at times. So, we'll need to adapt and trust that love will carry us through the toughest times. It always does.

As gardeners, we're figuring out how to grow our food and flowers in an ever-changing environment. We stay open to what is happening in the moment and create our gardens accordingly. This is adaptable gardening, and, in the future, the healthiest gardens will be those based in cooperation, in which gardens and gardeners alike choose to evolve in tandem, learning how to work with the joys—and sometimes challenges—of gardening on a planet in the midst of climate change.

PRACTICAL INFORMATION FOR GARDENING IN CLIMATE CHANGE

So, with all this new information, what's a gardener to do? First, it's very important to cultivate a good attitude. Be curious about climate change and study how it's affecting your area. Learn to flow with a changing climate instead of fighting against it. Be adaptable. In seed and plant selection, you might think about choosing new varieties that are more tolerant of weather extremes. If you save seed, sow your own seeds. Those seeds will produce plants that have already adapted to your unique gardening climate, and they'll be more resilient than any seeds or plants you might buy.

In some areas, you might be able to take advantage of a longer growing season than you're used to experiencing in your garden. If that's the case, you could plant successive vegetable crops in your extended season—the first planted in spring and the second in midsummer. You might also take advantage of earlier planting dates if your spring is warm. Just be diligent concerning spring frosts, and protect your plants accordingly. You might invest in frost cloth or mini plastic greenhouses; both can be placed over tender seedlings if the spring weather gets nasty.

It's important to be flexible with your yearly pruning schedule. During warmer winters, an early pruning of your fruit trees, roses, and garden perennials works just fine. But in colder years, it's best to allow the plants to remain dormant and prune them later in the season, possibly not so hard. Again, it's important to be adaptable in all that you do in the garden.

If you live in an area that is affected by a shortage of water, it's important to improve your water-management practice. First, it's a good thing to build healthy soil using plenty of organic matter, such as manures, leaves, and so on. This allows better water-holding capacity and drainage. It's also good to increase your water-wise irrigation capacity by installing a good drip system, volume drip emitters, and irrigation timers. The timers can be programmed for morning or evening watering to avoid midday evaporation. Mulching the garden will also help the soil retain its moisture and protect the sensitive roots of plants, especially during periods of excessive summer heat.

If you live in an area in which perennials from Mediterranean climates do well, those plants will make a fine addition to your garden. They are more adaptable to climate change, require less water, and thrive in the warm summer heat. Some of these include lavender, rosemary, sage, catmint, oregano, and thyme. Also, the herb Agastache flowers nonstop through the summer and is a bee and hummingbird magnet. (It thrives in heat too!)

The pollinators are adapting to a changing climate just like we are. Our gardens can be a lifesaver for them, especially if a change in the environment brings on an earlier-than-normal spring bloom or there are fewer blooms because of drought. This is especially true for migrating hummingbirds, who depend on the availability of flowers all along their route. Our garden flowers may provide much-needed fuel so the birds can continue their journey. As the flowering cycles change with the climate, the hummers and other pollinators need extra help from us. Our gardens can become way stations for them and for other wildlife too.

Another consideration in the garden, in light of climate change, is whether you want to cultivate a grassy lawn or not. According to a NASA study on lawns, fifty thousand square miles of grass covers the United States, which, according to EPA estimates, accounts for one-third of Americans' water usage. Since 95 percent of American lawns consist of Kentucky bluegrass, which is a thirsty grass, this figure is not surprising. There are alternatives to this, and if you want a lawn, you've got some great water-thrifty grasses to choose from. You need to determine whether cool- or warm-season grass is best for your location, and remember that the key to healthy grass is to promote deep roots through deep watering. Drought-resistant grass doesn't need to be watered often, but when it does, it needs to be watered deeply.

Depending on where you live, here are a few grasses to choose from.

1. Zoysia grass—This grass is flexible, loves sun and shade, and is slow growing. It tolerates traffic and produces a lush carpet. The most drought-resistant varieties are Palisades, Jamur, El Toro, and Empire.
2. St. Augustine grass—This grass generally prefers dappled shade. The most drought-tolerant variety is Floratum.
3. Buffalo grass—This is a Midwest prairie native. It needs full sun. It is a warm-season grass, but it tolerates cold. It also tolerates light traffic. It is a slow grower and has low rainfall requirements. Most varieties are drought tolerant.
4. Fescue—These are cool-season grasses for more northern climates. They absorb water well after drought.
5. Bahia grass—This is a decent choice for infertile soil. It needs full sun, and it is coarse, but it's thick covering. It is also drought tolerant.

If you are planning on creating a new lawn, you need only to do the soil work and plant the seeds or grass turf. But if you are replacing your existing thirsty lawn with one of the drought-resistant varieties of grass (or you are getting rid of your lawn all together), you have two choices on how to get rid of the existing grass—digging or smothering it. Using chemical poisons is *not* an option, of course!

First, though, before you begin the grass removal, it's important to honor the existing lawn for its life and for what it has given to you and the garden. Sit with the grass and ask to be connected to the Devas, Nature Spirits, and any other beings connected to the grass. Explain what you plan to do and why. Keep it simple, as Nature understands when we speak from the heart. Thank the grass, send it your love, and welcome its spirit to continue on in the garden in whatever form it would like to take on its journey. Maybe it would like to be part of the new lawn or the vegetable or flower garden. It's so important to honor all of Nature in the garden, even what you are planning to kill. The love you carry in your heart speaks volumes, and your garden will feel it.

Once you are complete with this process, it's time to decide which method you want to use to remove the grass. You can either dig it up or smother it using newspaper or plastic. Digging up the lawn means you won't have any of the old grass left to deal with, provided you dig deep and sift the dirt well, catching any straggler roots that might have remained buried in the soil. But if you would rather smother the grass than dig it up, know that the process takes longer; you might have to repeat it a few times to make sure you've killed all the grass roots.

If you decide to smother the grass, one option is to use newspaper. Start by mowing the area, which allows the newspaper to lay flatter and closer to the grass. Wet the area and begin placing thick layers of newspaper (about eight to ten sheets) over the grass, overlapping in different directions as you go. You may want to continue wetting the area to prevent the newspaper from blowing away. Once the area is completely covered, add mulch or landscape fabric. As no light will penetrate the area, the grass will eventually smother and die. This process takes at least two weeks.

If you decide to use plastic, mow the grassy area first and cover it with black plastic. Unlike clear plastic, the black color will block out the light, smothering grass roots and preventing new growth. Secure the plastic and allow it to remain in place for a few weeks or even longer depending on the size of the lawn. After the grass has died, dig it up and prepare the soil for your new plantings, whatever they may be.

We have a small lawn here that helps to keep the house cool in the summer, plus cats, kids, and big kids love to lounge on it. Our lawn is full of clover, so the bees love it, and all kinds of insects enjoy it when it's wet. The dragonflies love the grass too, as they fly and hover, catching the tiny insects attracted to the moisture. Our lawn is also a working lawn, as we use the grass clippings every summer to add to the compost. I don't advocate having a big lawn, but a small one is perfect, as it serves many critters and people too.

There are many folks who advocate getting rid of a lawn all together. In its place, they're planting edible gardens full of herbs, vegetables, and flowers. Many front yards are now garden plots, and it's fun to see all the food being grown where grass once was. Other folks have chosen to replace their grass with a native garden full of flowers, which is highly beneficial for the wildlife in the area. Whatever you choose, whether you replace your lawn with drought-resistant grass, downsize it to a small patch of turf, or even replace it with edibles and flowers, it's all good to do in the midst of a changing climate. The more we embrace the change and find ways to work with it in our own gardens and in our lives, the better off we'll be and the more we'll contribute to the overall health of the planet. Adaptable gardening is the way of the future. We need to flow with this new way of gardening and incorporate it into everything we do, including how and when we work our soil, plant our seeds, tend our crops, and harvest our bounty. The Earth is speaking to us in each and every moment, and all we need to do is to cultivate an open heart, a flexible mind, and the willingness to listen.

Twelve

An Introduction to Flower Essences

*If we could see
the miracle of a single
flower clearly,
our whole life would change.*

—Buddha

What is a flower essence? It is a vibrational remedy, similar to homeopathic remedies, that provides healing and balancing in a subtle yet powerful way. A flower essence is not an herbal extract. Herbal extracts heal through direct biochemical interaction within the physiology of the body. In other words, they heal on a physical level. Flower essences work on a vibrational level. Each flower essence embodies the healing signature of the particular flower from which it was made. Flower essences are created by placing a flower (or flowers) in a bowl of water and allowing it to sit in the sun for about three or four hours, which allows the specific healing and balancing pattern contained within the flower petals to be released into the water. The water has thus been potentized and is now ready for use.

Early research on flower essences was conducted in the twentieth century by an English physician named Edward Bach. He developed a set of thirty-eight essences, which he used to treat the underlying emotional patterns that were the cause of physical disorders and disease in his patients. One of his most popular and highly effective formulas, known as Rescue Remedy, is widely used as a first response for shock or trauma in both humans and animals.

How do flower essences work to help us heal? As a vibrational remedy, they work directly with the electrical and central nervous systems. Our bodies have, within them and surrounding them, an electrical network. This network remains balanced and fully connected when we are healthy, but when something interrupts that balance, the electrical system responds by either short-circuiting or overloading. This, in turn, impacts the central nervous system, and the body goes into high gear in an effort to correct the imbalance. If it doesn't succeed, then we physically manifest the imbalance, whether through illness or through various body ailments such as headaches, backaches, or neck pain. By taking the flower essences that best align with our needs, we immediately balance the electrical system, which stabilizes the nervous system and helps the body to move from a state of "dis-ease" to a state of balance and ease. So, how do we choose the essence(s) we need for our healing? The best way is to do your research. Read about the various flower essences that are available. See which essence or essences are a close match to what you may need, and choose accordingly. Besides the well-known Bach Flower Remedies, there are many other flower essence companies to choose from. You might consider finding a flower-essence practitioner (of which I am one) to create a personal remedy that is made just for you. This takes the guesswork out of choosing the essences you'll need for your healing. In my practice, I've created (along with the Devas, of course) fifty essences, and I use them to create remedies for myself and my clients. I receive angelic and devic guidance to choose which essences will be best for the healing and balancing that I need and that my clients need. Each practitioner has her own unique way of creating essence blends for her clients, and I'm sure you'll be led to the practitioner that is just right for you. You can also step it up a notch, so to speak, by creating your own unique collection of flower essences. You'll find that, with trust and an open mind, you'll be naturally drawn to the perfect flowers to use for your health and well-being. And if you grow the flowers yourself, the connection will be even stronger!

So, now we'll begin the essence-making process. Therefore, you'll have the opportunity to experience firsthand how to make them for yourself.

In the morning light, we gather our chosen flowers, placing them in a clear, clean bowl of water. Only a few are needed to make an essence. Depending on the flower size, anywhere from one to five flowers is perfect. We choose flowers that haven't fully opened yet. This way they release their full potency into the water as they open to the sun instead of having already released their energy into the environment. We use clean scissors and snip the flowers directly into the bowl. We do it this way so that our personal energy doesn't become part of the mix by touching the flowers. Standing—or kneeling—by the bowl of floating flowers, we place our hands, palms up, on either side of the bowl. We connect with the faeries and devas of the garden (we ask to be connected so they may assist us in the essence-making process), and then request that "the healing and balancing pattern contained within the flowers may be infused into the water at this time." It's a joy to feel the healing energy as it releases into the water, but even if you don't feel it like I do, it still happens instantly. You can trust that. It's important that we allow about thirty seconds or so before we remove our hands from the sides of the bowl. This allows the etheric release to ground fully into the water. Then, it's always nice to bring our hands together in prayer, blessing the flowers, the garden helpers, and ourselves for bringing this beautiful healing essence into being. Next, it's time to ground the essence physically through its interaction with the light energy of the sun. We leave the bowls in the garden for about three or four hours, covering each bowl with a piece of cheesecloth to keep the essence water free of insects. If we are making more than one essence at a time, we repeat the process for each one, placing the bowls together on a table (or on the ground) and making sure they don't touch each other. When we return later in the day, we bring the bowls inside and remove the flowers with clean tweezers, making sure to avoid touching the water with our hands. We then pour the water into clean glass jars or bottles. (Don't forget to label them.) Sometimes it's helpful to use a small measuring cup for this process, especially if the mouth of the jar is small. We preserve the essence with brandy, using a ratio of 40 percent brandy to 60 percent essence water. (Some folks use vinegar instead of brandy.) This increases the shelf life of the essence. Otherwise it will spoil quickly, as it contains residue from plant material. Once the bottles or jars are filled, we can put them either someplace special to us in the garden or next to some crystals, for instance, to sit awhile. This allows the essence and preservative to coalesce into one stable unit. Once that's complete, we take each mother tincture, as they're called, dilute it down with water and brandy (or vinegar), and put them into dosage bottles. I've found that either two-dram or half-ounce dropper bottles are good sizes to use. I use a company called Specialty Bottle Company to buy all my bottles, and they've been a reliable company for years. To dilute the essence down, we put a few drops of mother tincture and a few drops of preservative into the dosage bottle, fill it with clean water, and label it.

Next, it's time to receive the healing definitions for the essences that we've made. Holding each bottle, we connect with the devas and faeries who would like to assist in the process, and we ask to be given the definition for "the healing and balancing pattern" contained in each essence. It's important to write down any impressions you receive without censoring them, whether you see, feel, or hear something. Stay with the process until it feels like you have a clear definition for each essence. For example, when I asked for the healing pattern of my pink rose, Bewitched, I was shown a picture of a pink baby blanket, and I had a feeling of being all snuggled into that blanket. So, the definition was that this essence helps to give a feeling of nurturing and security, like being all snuggled up in a warm blanket. In the years since I received that definition, the Bewitched rose essence has, indeed, proven to be a comforting remedy. There's no rule on how long or short the definitions need to be. Just trust the process on what you receive, and write it down. With practice, the process gets easier.

When the essence-making process is complete, thank everyone again for their assistance and close the connection. Store the bottles or jars in a cool, dry place. Because they've been preserved, they will last for many years to come.

MAKING GEM ELIXIRS

A gem elixir carries the specific healing qualities of the gemstone that is used to make it. Folks have been using gemstones and crystals for healing for years with good results, and much has been written on the subject.

The process of making gem elixirs is similar to making a flower essence in that you place the gemstone in a bowl of water and leave it in the sun for a few hours to potentize the water. Make sure the gemstones you use are not toxic when ingested. There are so many gemstones to choose from. Rose quartz and amethyst are two of my favorites, but see what calls to you.

To make the elixir, place the gemstone you have chosen in a clear, clean bowl of water. Use a clean utensil such as a spoon to place the gemstone in the water so you don't mix your personal energy into the elixir. Connect with the Devas, Faeries, or anyone else who wants to be part of the process, and with your hands on either side of the bowl (palms up), ask that "the healing and balancing pattern of the gemstone be infused into the water at this time." Allow the etheric release to ground for about thirty seconds, and then remove your hands and leave the bowl in the sun for about three or four hours to ground the elixir physically. After that, remove the gemstone and bottle the elixir up, again using brandy or vinegar to preserve it. This time the ratio should be 80 percent elixir to 20 percent brandy. Ask the Devas for the healing definition that is personal for you, and then disconnect from their energy, thanking them for their assistance. Gem elixirs are powerful remedies and make a good addition to your medicine chest.

MAKING ENVIRONMENTAL ESSENCES

Environmental essences capture a particular environment at the time they are made. Good examples of this are essences made on solstice or equinox cycles, those made on full- or new-moon cycles, or even those that capture the energies of sacred sites around the world.

We'll use the example of how to make an environmental essence for the spring equinox, and then you can expand from there.

First, fill a clean bowl with water and connect with the energies of the sun, the Earth, and any other Nature beings that want to be part of the process. At the exact time of the spring equinox (which you can find in the *Farmers' Almanac* or on an astrological calendar), place your hands on either side of the bowl (palms up) and ask that "the energy of the spring equinox be infused into the water at this time." You might want to focus on what the energy of spring means to you. Maybe it's about the rebirth of life, as grass grows and flowers bloom, baby animals are born, and the sun moves higher in the sky each day. Stay with the feeling as it is captured in the water, and when you feel complete with the process, thank all who have assisted and leave the bowl to sit in the energy awhile. When it feels like the water is fully potentized with the energy of spring, you can bottle it up—20 percent preservative to 80 percent essence water—and ask for the healing definition from those who have assisted in the process. Thank them all again and disconnect. You now have the energy of spring in a bottle, so enjoy!

SUPPLY LIST FOR MAKING ESSENCES AND ELIXIRS

- clean glass bowls (they should hold about 5 cups of water)
- clean filtered water
- clean glass jars to store essences (½ qt. to 1 qt. size)
- clean tweezers
- clean spoon for gem elixirs
- clean glass measuring cup
- clean glass dropper bottles (½ oz. or 2 dram size)
- brandy or vinegar, organic if possible
- labels and pen to use for labeling jars and dropper bottles

Flowers are
vibrating strings
in a
symphony of light!

Garden Rainbows Essences

I offer four essence kits made from my garden flowers and gemstones. Each kit includes five essences that embody a particular theme. These themes include *joy, personal power, comfort, and transformation.* The essences are in one-dram amber glass dropper bottles, and they're placed in a velvet drawstring pouch. Below is the list of essences found in each kit.

JOY

- *Larkspur—Singing with Joy!*
- *Cherry—Delight*
- *Mexican Sunflower—Exuberance*
- *Rose Quartz—Heart Opening*
- *Nectarine—Sweetness of Life*

PERSONAL POWER

- *Rosemary—Grounded with Clarity*
- *Carrot—Solid in Oneself*
- *Chrysler Imperial Rose—Strength*
- *Dill—Personal Power*
- *Honor Rose—Honor Thyself*

COMFORT

- *Bewitched Rose—Nurturing*
- *Tulip—Cup of Comfort*
- *Yarrow—Protective Light*
- *Scabiosa—Softness*
- *Honey Perfume—Soothing*

TRANSFORMATION

- *Heaven on Earth—Balance*
- *Amethyst—Deep Cleansing and Transformation*
- *Iris—Clear Vision and Third-Eye Opening*
- *California Poppy—Rebirth*
- *Cabana Rose—Full Sails Ahead: Wings to Fly!*

The price for each kit is $30.00 plus $4.95 shipping and handling, and they can be ordered through my website at GardenRainbows.com. I also offer a **Custom-Blend Essence**, which I create intuitively for each client. Through tuning into my guides and angels as well as those of my clients, I choose the essences that will best serve their needs at the time. These are blended together in a healing remedy. I also receive a message of healing and understanding that is personal to them, and I include this with the remedy. I have fifty of my own personal essences to choose from in making a blend, and most remedies use anywhere from three to six essences, whatever is needed. The custom-blend essence is in a half-ounce green dropper bottle, and the cost is $25.00 plus $4.95 shipping and handling. Because this is a personal blend, it is important to connect either through e-mail or a phone call before the essence is made. In the United States, either will work; outside the United States, only e-mail will work. My contact information is found on my website at GardenRainbows.com.

BRAND NEW! GARDEN BALANCE ESSENCE KIT

The essence blends in this kit have been created to assist our gardens in achieving a state of balance. Because our gardens are our reflections, we can also use them to balance our bodies and our lives. To use them in the garden, we can hand sprinkle them; use a watering can, spray mister, or handheld pump sprayer; or even place a few drops in an open palm and ask the garden energies to take what is needed. They are quite effective this way. For ourselves, we can take a few drops under the tongue, spray a diluted mix on our bodies, or place a few drops in our bathwater and let it soak in. To discern which essence blend is needed for you or the garden, you can use your intuition by placing your hand on your heart and feeling the answer or by holding each essence to your solar plexus to discern if it's needed or not. A pendulum works well for this too.

GARDEN LIGHT

This essence enlivens the entire garden with health and vitality. It works with the plants, trees, Nature Spirits, and Garden Devas. The blend consists of

- *Electron Rose—Energy*
- *Cherry—Delight*
- *Dill—Personal Power*
- *Larkspur—Singing with Joy!*

FAERIE DANCE

This essence brings lightness and joy to the garden. It works with the Faerie Realm and the flowers in the garden. The blend consists of

- *Echinacea—Deep Healing on All Levels*
- *Lilac—Fresh Perspective*
- *Tropicana Rose—Contentment: The Buddha Essence!*
- *Electron Rose—Energy*

ANIMAL SPEAK

This essence helps to support and balance the animal life in the garden, those that live there as well as those just passing through. The blend consists of

- *Christopher Marlowe Rose—Refreshing*
- *Dill—Personal Power*
- *Bewitched Rose—Nurturing*
- *Parry's Agave—Resilience*

SOIL TALK

This essence brings balance to the soil, rocks, and crystals in the garden. It works with and assists the Gnomes, Soil Elementals, Soil Microbes, and Soil Devas. The blend consists of

- *Electron Rose—Energy*
- *Almond—Lightness of Being*
- *Rosa Poppy—Free 'n Easy!*
- *California Poppy—Rebirth*

GOOD DAY SUNSHINE!

This essence helps to clear and balance the atmosphere of the garden. It works with the Weather Devas, the Air and Water Elementals, and the Sun. The blend consists of

- *Fall Equinox—Begin Again*
- *Cabana Rose—Full Sails Ahead: Wings to Fly!*
- *Iris—Clear Vision and Third-Eye Opening*
- *Peach—Fullness of Being*

The price for the Garden Essence Balance Kit is $35.00 plus $4.95 shipping and handling.

Thirteen

A Meditation for You

*Your light
reminds others
of their light.*

—Emmanuel

*Y*ou're probably wondering what meditation is doing in a gardening book. My answer to you is…*every-thing*! A more balanced gardener creates a more balanced garden. It's that simple. Anyone can medi-tate. It crosses all boundaries, all cultures, and all faiths. All of life is energy, including us, and meditation helps to smooth out our energy and keep us healthy. The meditation I'm sharing with you is part of my daily practice. It has become an integral part of my life. Often, when I begin to meditate, I feel scattered or maybe even a bit ungrounded. By the time I finish, however, I'm centered, grounded, and peaceful. If this practice resonates with you, you can incorporate it into your daily life. Of course, there are many other meditation practices available, and all can be highly beneficial for your health and well-being. You'll be drawn to the right practice for you, whether it's this one or another, so trust the process. Meditation will bring a state of balance and health to your life; it certainly has to mine.

The method I'm teaching here is a chakra-balancing meditation. The word *chakra* is a Sanskrit word meaning "spinning vortex" or "wheel." Each of us has a main channel of energy that runs through the center of the body. This channel has many names, such as the pranic tube, divine line, or column of light. The energy that flows into the top of the tube is cosmic energy; it is high-frequency energy. The energy that flows up into the tube from below is Earth energy, which is heavier and maintains our balance with the Earth. These two energies meet in the middle at the solar plexus chakra (which is about two inches above the navel). From there, they are mixed and distributed through the chakra and meridian systems (think acupuncture). The flow of energy is fed through the chakras first and then further distributed throughout the meridian system. There are seven major chakras in the body and many other minor chakras. The seven major chakras begin at the base of the spine and move upward to the crown of the head. They coincide with the positions along the spinal cord at which the major nerve ganglia connect. The chakras take in the energy, metabolize it, and send it to the major nerve plexus area closest to the chakra. From there, it moves out along the appropriate energy meridian and across the field of the physical body. This energy is very important for the healthy functioning of the physical self. If a chakra isn't functioning properly, the body organs and other parts served by that chakra will not get the supply of energy they need to stay healthy. That part of the body will weaken, as will its immune defenses, and this can lead to disease. That's why it's so important to keep the chakras open and balanced in their spin.

A healthy chakra is shaped a bit like a cone or pyramid. Within the cone (or pyramid) is a vortex of energy that normally rotates clockwise. Through the rotation (or spin) of the chakra, energy is drawn up from the central column (the pranic tube) and distributed throughout the chakra's respective area of the body. This rotating energy is where the name chakra (or spinning vortex) originated.

The first chakra is known as the root, or base, chakra. It is located at the base of the spine in the tailbone area. It is related to the will to live and supplies the body with physical vitality. It also supplies energy to the spinal column, the adrenals, and the kidneys.

The second chakra is known as the sacral chakra. It is located in the lower abdomen about two inches below the navel. It is related to sensuality and sexuality and to our creative abilities in the world. It supplies energy to the sexual organs and immune system.

The third chakra is known as the solar-plexus chakra. It is located in the upper abdomen area. It is associated with intuition—our gut instincts and with personal power in the world. It relates to who we are in the universe and how we connect to others. It supplies the organs in this area of the body with their energies—the stomach, liver, gall bladder, pancreas, spleen, and nervous system.

The fourth chakra is known as the heart chakra. This chakra works with love in all its forms. It is located in the center of the chest, just above the physical heart. It brings energy to the heart, circulatory system, thymus, vagus nerve, and upper back.

The fifth chakra is known as the throat chakra. It is located in the soft part of the throat. It is related to giving, receiving, and speaking our truth. It supplies energy to the thyroid, bronchi, lungs, and alimentary canal.

The sixth chakra is known as the third-eye, or brow, chakra. It is located in the forehead, just above the nose and between the two physical eyes. It is associated with the senses of sight. It pertains to "seeing" what we need to do and then carrying out our ideas step-by-step to accomplish them. It supplies energy to the pituitary, lower brain, left eye, ears, nose, and nervous system.

The seventh chakra is known as the crown chakra. It is located at the top of the head and is associated with the experience of direct knowing and the integration of personality with spirituality. It supplies energy to the upper brain and right eye.

Each chakra (except for the root and the crown) has a front and a back aspect to its function. The front correlates to emotional functioning—our feelings—and the back to our will. Together they make up a complete energy circuit, creating a balance of feeling and will in each chakra center.

So, now with the basic understanding of how the chakra system functions as well as of the importance of keeping the system balanced and healthy, we'll move on to the meditation.

Chakra-Balancing Meditation

Begin by finding a comfortable place to sit or lie down, someplace where you won't be disturbed. With eyes open, start breathing slowly and focus your attention on a point directly in front of you. It could be a chair, a light, a bush, or a tree; it doesn't matter. Take three breaths as you focus on the point you have chosen. Then close your eyes, still focusing on this point. See the image in your mind's eye. Take three more breaths with eyes closed, focusing on the point. This allows you to enter the meditative state quietly. Your focus on a single object quiets the normal mind chatter as it creates a smooth transition from open eyes to closed eyes. Spend a little time here before you move on.

Now, let the focal point fade away and bring your awareness to the top of the head at your crown chakra. Ask the crown to open to receive the universal (or cosmic) energy that flows in from above and all around you. Feel this golden-white light as it bathes your crown. Breathe the light into the chakra, with each breath pulling in more light. Stay with this for several breaths, and feel your crown as it fills with the light. When it feels full and radiant, move down through the crown and flood your brain with the golden-white light. Feel it enlivening your brain, glowing with energy, and filling your pituitary, pineal, and hypothalamus glands. Now, direct the light to your third-eye (brow) chakra. Breathe and feel the chakra open as it fills with golden-white light. Continue to move the light throughout your head; fill your eyes, your nose, your mouth, and your ears with the golden-white light. From there, breathe the light down your neck to the soft spot in the throat. Open and fill the throat chakra with this beautiful light. Once your throat feels full and open, move down into your chest area. See your beautiful heart as it rests between your lungs, which are like wings enfolding your precious heart. Breathe the golden-white light into the heart chakra, just above the physical heart. Let the light expand through the heart and the lungs, out the shoulders, down the arms, and out through the hands. Feel the light streaming through the palms and out the fingertips. Feel the light expanding the love in your heart. You have so much to give, so much to receive, so much to be as you fill with golden light. Stay with this for a few moments until your heart feels full. Next, move down to the solar plexus. See this chakra as a beautiful shining sun. Breathe the golden-white light into your solar plexus sun and watch it grow brighter. This is your personal power center. Feel its radiance as it fills with the golden-white light. From there, move down to the sacral chakra, just below the navel. This is the womb of your creativity. All life is born here. Fill this chakra with the golden-white light, and see it as a chrysalis, in which the butterflies of your creations are born to fly. When this chakra is full, breathe the light into the first chakra; breathe down into your root. This root is your center of vitality and well-being. Ground this center with golden-white light. Breathe in your connection to the Earth, to the root of who you are.

When this chakra feels full and grounded, it's time to move the golden-white light down into the Earth. Create a grounding cord, attached to your tailbone, and send it down into the center of the Earth. It can be a root, a cord, a rope, a tail—whatever image works for you is fine. Drop it down into the Earth; no matter where you are, the cord will find its way. Breathe the golden-white light down the cord into the center of the Earth, the heart of Gaia. She will receive the light gladly, a special gift from you. Stay with this for a bit as you feel the connection you have with the soul of the Earth. You are the conduit as you unite Heaven with Earth, and the energy becomes a blend of the two. When you are ready, you can begin to loop this blended energy back through your body, starting at your feet. Each foot has a chakra at its sole, and you can visualize each of these chakras opening like a camera lens, drawing the light through them, into your feet, up your legs, and into the first chakra—into your root. See the golden-white light fill your root chakra, and as you feel it enlivening this chakra, say (out loud or to yourself), "I am fully grounded to the Earth, grounded in love and light." Feel the light as you breathe its energy throughout your first chakra. When the chakra feels full, move the golden-white light up into the second chakra. Breathe its energy into the sacral center, filling it with beautiful light, and say, "I am creating my life with love and light." Feel the energy fill your second chakra. When it is full, breathe the golden-white light into the third chakra. Feel the light as it fills your solar plexus chakra, and say, "I am me. I am the power of love and light." Feel the warmth and brightness as you fill your third chakra with this golden light, and when it's full, move up to the fourth chakra—your sacred heart. Breathe the light into your beautiful heart—the center of your being—and say, "I am the heart; I am the center of love and light." Sit with this for a moment as the light expands through your heart, filling your whole chest with radiant light. When your heart is full, move up to the fifth chakra and breathe the light energy into your throat, filling it with beautiful golden-white light. Feel your throat center open as you say, "I speak my truth with love and light." Feel the words resonate through this chakra. When it is full of light, move up to the sixth chakra. Breathe the energy into the third-eye center, filling it with golden-white light. As you feel the light fill your sixth chakra, say, "My vision is clear and true; I see with love and light." Feel this light awakening your vision even more, and when it is full, move up to the seventh chakra— your crown—and fill it with golden-white light. Breathe this beautiful energy all through your crown, and say, "I *am* love and light!" Feel the light energy as it flows out through your crown like a fountain, cascading down all around you. Bathe in this light, and breathe deeply from the center of your being. When you are full, bring your focus back to your third eye. In your mind's eye, see a point of light shining at the center of your forehead. With eyes closed, focus on this point as you take three breaths. On the third breath, open your eyes. Still focusing on the point of light, slowly bring your focus back to the world around you. Sit in the stillness for a moment as you come back to your outer reality. Take a few more grounding breaths, and carry this balance into your day.

Quick Reference Guide for Chakra Meditation

- **Sit or lie down—get comfortable.**
- **Eyes open, focus on a point. Take three smooth breaths as you breathe your eyes closed, still focusing on the point.**
- **Bring awareness to the crown chakra. Open the chakra to receive universal energy. Bathe in this light.**
- **Flood the brain with light. Direct it to the brow (third-eye) chakra and bathe in the universal light.**
- **Breathe the energy down your neck and into the soft spot in the throat. Bathe the throat chakra with universal light.**
- **See your beautiful heart as it rests between the lungs. Bathe your heart chakra (just above the physical heart) with the universal light. Expand the light into the shoulders, down the arms, and out the palms and fingertips. Stay with this awhile, until your heart feels full.**
- **Bring the universal energy into your solar plexus—your own personal sun center—and fill it with radiant light.**
- **Flood your sacral chakra (just below the navel) with the universal energy. Feel this center of your creativity as it fills with light.**
- **Move the universal energy into your base-root chakra and see it fill with light.**
- **Create a grounding cord, connecting it first to your tailbone and then dropping it down to the Earth.**
- **Move the universal energy down the grounding cord, filling the Earth with light. Stay with this awhile and breathe as the energy runs through your body, connecting heaven to Earth.**
- **Loop the energy back from the Earth through the body, first opening the chakras in the feet and then directing the energy through each foot chakra as it moves up the legs into the first chakra.**
- **Fill the first chakra with light, and say, "I am fully grounded to the Earth, grounded in love and light."**
- **From there, fill the second chakra with light, and say, "I am creating my life with love and light."**
- **Next, fill the third chakra with light, and say, "I am me. I am the power of love and light."**

- From there, fill the fourth chakra with light, and say, "I am the heart; I am the center of love and light." Feel your heart as it becomes totally full with this beautiful energy.
- Next, fill the fifth chakra with light, and say, "I speak my truth with love and light."
- From there, fill the sixth chakra with light, and say, "My vision is clear and true. I see with love and light."
- Finally, move into the seventh chakra. Fill the crown with light, and say, "I *am* love and light." Feel the energy flow out through your crown like a fountain, cascading down all around you.
- When you are full, bring your focus to your third eye; see the point of light in the center of your forehead. Focus on this point, take three smooth breaths, and open your eyes, still focusing on the point of light.
- Slowly bring your focus back into your world, take a few more grounding breaths, and carry this balance into your day.

Fourteen

An Attitude of Reverence

Plant kindness
and gather
love.

—Proverb

What does it mean to practice reverence in the garden? How can we be lovingly mindful in each moment as we water, weed, feed, harvest, and tend to all the needs of the garden? It's a question worth asking, and I'll do my best to give a good answer.

In a cocreative garden, the needs of the gardener and the garden have equal voice. It's not just about what we receive from the garden, whether it's fruits, vegetables, or flowers, but it's also about what we give back to the garden as we create a happy and healthy garden environment. We know that when the garden is happy and healthy, its bountiful gifts flow easily back to us, and everyone benefits.

It all begins with the seed. We choose organic heirloom seeds that are passed down through generations with love and care. When it's time to plant, we hold the precious seeds close to our hearts and bless them, asking the spirits of seed and soil to help them grow. Each seed is such a miracle! It contains the blueprint for roots, stems, leaves, blossoms, and fruit. With the fruit, the miracle begins again, as each piece contains the seeds for future planting.

At planting time, we gently tuck the seeds into good soil. The soil is rich with microbials, fungi, and earthworms, each playing a vital part in creating a healthy mix in which seeds can sprout and grow. Watering them in, we bless the gift of clean, precious water—Earth's lifeblood—as it nourishes seeds, plants, gardens, our bodies, and the Earth itself. All need water to survive and thrive.

As the garden matures, we continue to practice an attitude of reverence in all that we do. We are mindful and respectful when we trim the plants. We're grateful when we harvest the fruits and vegetables. When we have to weed, we bless the plants as we pull them up, honoring them for their lives, as all life is sacred.

It's all about love as we work in the garden—love in planting, tending, watering, weeding, harvesting, and even killing something. What we carry in our hearts is what moves through our gardens. It's that simple.

With the animals that live in the garden and those that occasionally pass through, it's important for us to create a balance between what we need and what they need, as all benefit from the garden's bounty. When problems arise with the animals or insects taking too much or weakening the plants with their foraging, how do we stay in a place of love while still taking the actions needed to remedy the situation? What if that means killing the insects, such as when Steve and I choose to use neem oil on the spider mites that often overrun and kill our bean plants? It seems to me that if we cultivate an attitude of reverence, of love, for *everything* we do in the garden (such as loving the spider mites, the bean plants, and the neem oil), our hearts remain open and true; Nature understands the truth of an open heart.

As gardeners and caretakers of the Earth, an open heart begins with us. How much do we love ourselves? How much do we treat ourselves with an attitude of reverence? We can only love another to the degree that we can love ourselves, and often our gardens reflect this truth back to us. An issue with the garden may be showing us where we need to love and take care of ourselves more. Are there insects swarming on your tender lettuce? Are animals digging in your flower beds? Is the garden reflecting back to you where you are feeling vulnerable or victimized in your own life? Pay attention to the messages you receive from the garden. Do what you need to do for the garden, such as covering the lettuce or putting up fences around the flower beds. But also do what you need to do for *you*, such as creating a healthy boundary so others can't take advantage of you or drain your energy. When you address your needs as well as the needs of the garden, a state of balance is achieved and the end result is a happier garden and a happier you. If you continue to see the garden as your reflection, you will learn much about yourself, and through taking healthy actions when issues arise, you and your garden will thrive.

An attitude of reverence begins with a single heart. When that single heart opens to love, it touches many more hearts, until all hearts are open, radiating with love and light. Because we're one with the Earth, she too radiates that love back to us, and our lives on Earth forever change. What a beautiful world it is as the Earth becomes the Garden of Eden she was always meant to be. This new paradise on Earth begins where the story always begins—in the garden.

3.

Part III
Conversations with Nature

A Morning Spent with a Butterfly

I came to you today to be the first conversation for the book. I wanted to be a part of your book, a part of your conversation. I am, indeed, the embodiment of transformation. Not only do I speak to you on your personal journey, but also I embody the template of transformation for the Earth itself.

As a world traveler, I connect the dots, seeding my unique energies into many places. It is what I carry and what I am here to do.

So many love my dance, fluttering about, carefree, flying among the flowers with wings in shades of autumn leaves. A blend of polka dots and lines, I am a creator's artwork in perfect design.

I fear nothing; I live with whatever comes my way—wind, heat, sun, cold, and rain. I hunker down with the harshness and bask in the warmth when the sunny days return. I go with the flow, as all of Nature does. We adapt to what is, and we teach you to do the same.

You, my friend, are learning this too. You are learning to adapt and be flexible, and that is why I came to you today. I am here so you can fully embody my energy, as I am enjoying yours. You are a child of the Earth, of the light, and your sweet nature flows out to everyone. Your love and care for nature and the garden is felt by all, and we bask in it.

You are in the midst of a huge transformation, dear friend, and it is one step at a time for you.

Butterfly energy holds the template for that. Hold this in your heart, as we have shared our hearts this morning. Trust the process. Hunker down under a leaf when you need to rest. Flutter among the flowers when you need to fly. Enjoy your life and take it as it comes. Go with the flow. Trust the process. You and your world are transforming. Take my spirit with you on your travels; as you teach, as you learn, and as you grow, I will guide you. I offer softness and strength, embodied in one. I am with you always, in love.

—Melody

A Message from the Honeybees in the Garden
December 3, 2016

Thank you for greeting us, as we love to talk to you. Our message is a simple one for you today. We ask that you be adaptable. Accept what is. Go with the flow, especially in these times. Change what needs to be changed, and be brave. Most of all, be love. Let the love pour out of your cells, out of your being.

We live simple lives. We awaken, feel the day, and act accordingly. We are more simple by design than you are, but it would still serve you to follow this same way of being. Wake up in the morning and "taste" the flavor of your day. No matter what it looks like, fill it with your love, even before you get out of bed. In these times, that is what is needed, more than ever before.

Yes, we're aware of the shift that is happening. We feel it within the Earth as she radiates these changes. The song she sings informs us of what she's feeling in any moment, and we respond to that song. You can hear her song too. Walk barefoot in the sand, and her song will play through your feet if you listen. Smell a beautiful flower, and her notes will play through your senses. Wrap your arms around a tree and feel her song rise from the roots and embrace you. Root yourself in the Earth like a tree. Your body came from the Earth, and it feels safe there. Once you are rooted, life will be much easier. You'll know how to respond to your day, just like we do. Look to Nature as your guide. Love Nature as your friend. And live with Nature in a respectful way. That is what we ask of you now.

These changing times are hard for us—for all of us—but we in Nature celebrate them. And the Earth, Gaia, celebrates them too. The old way of being on the Earth is leaving, and what is coming is truly glorious! We can see it, and we wish we could somehow show all of humanity how radiant the Earth looks out there in the future.

We will get there, not those of us here now, but it will come eventually. We are the beginning—the way showers, the seed planters, the light gatherers, and the builders of this new world. Be patient, be open, and be love. That is what is needed in these times of great change. Be love, most of all.

We are loving you always,
The Honeybees

Sabrina and the Goats
by Mary Tannheimer

This story is involved, and it contains large concepts that have not been pondered by humans to any degree for millennia.

Sabrina lived in an area about a half hour north of Bishop that was swept through by a wildfire that destroyed many homes in the small community there. She had goats, along with many other animals, at her home and had to rescue them from the fire by driving the narrow, dirt back roads to her house. She skirted past and hid from law enforcement and fire personnel until she could pull out all her goats and other animals from their pens, load them into her vehicle, and drive away the same way she came in. She was absolutely not going to chance that they would be injured or killed in the fire. It was a good thing, because her home was destroyed. Her family and animals were safe, though.

Sabrina and her husband decided not to rebuild in the same community. They bought a house and property on the western edge of Bishop. They built new goat housing, with a pond and jumps for entertainment, and the chickens ran among the goats and sang to their heart's content. Four of the goats lived in a smaller area near the house, and one of these goats was pregnant. These were some of her special friends that had been rescued from the fire.

One day, Sabrina and her neighbors noticed mountain-lion tracks on the outside of the fence. They began to keep watch and let the dogs out more over the next several days to pressure the lion to leave the area. But Sabrina and her husband, Ted, had to go to a meeting one evening and left the dogs in the house so they wouldn't be outside alone. That's when disaster struck. The lion entered the pen with the four goats and killed them all, in a sort of frenzy of killing. The mountain lion also partially ate the unborn baby, leaving a horrific scene of bloody carnage to be discovered by Sabrina and Ted when they came home that evening.

Sabrina called me about a week later, after she had had some time to grieve, and wanted to know why this gruesome and heart-wrenching event had happened. I went to her property, went into the pen, sat on a pine stump, and was quiet.

Goats: "Hello, how are you?"
Mary: "I'm not sure. This is a hard thing that has happened here."
Goats: "It seems so, yes. There was a reason, though."

The goats told me their deaths were fast and there was very little suffering. They knew beforehand that they all needed to die together, and they decided that death by lion would serve their purpose. They put out a call for a lion to come but were refused several times because the various lions didn't want to do that much killing all at the same time. They felt it was not a true representation of their kind and were not comfortable with what they perceived the consequences would be from humans to lions in general. Finally, a lion (a female energy, but not necessarily a female in form—this was not clear to me) answered, and she agreed to conduct the killings. This lion had thought about the requirements of the killing for several days and had talked to the goats awhile, because it was not a usual request with regard to the number of animals to be killed. She had come several times to look over the area and the goats (hence the days of footprints). This lion had considered serial killing before but had never done it. She was fearful yet fascinated by the concept. She knew the other lions did not approve of this type of killing, so she hid out in seclusion, debating her choices. She finally agreed. Per the goats' request, she waited to kill until all relevant humans were gone from the area for more than enough time to do all the killing. She was kept informed of this time frame by the goats. The goats said they had to leave as a unit because they help each other on other planes and together represent a complete energy. The lion killing them together was the only way they knew of to all leave at the same time.

The goats told me they had to go. They are preparing for a reentry. They represent something very old, and "you can't bring any of the old with you." Goats have been around for a *long* time (they were one of the first human domestics), and their genetics hold a lot of ancient human values. This unit struggled against this programming; with "Sabrina's help and big love," they took a different, more light-filled program back to "*goat.*" Many animals are doing this because life is changing on this planet, and "the old can't come along." Most of these changes are not physically visible yet, but in a few years they will start to show. The unit will return and reform after that. Sabrina will know them again.

Goats: "Please tell Sabrina this. Please do not be bitter or fearful because of what has happened. You have a beautiful place full of joy. This small place has a direct line into the heart of the Earth, and she treasures your connection. This was a special incident that we asked for, and we are so sorry this has hurt you so. We knew it would and had trouble deciding to actually go through with it, but we had to. We couldn't say no. Our evolution is too important, as is yours. The "larger you" chose to accept this event because it furthers all things on this planet and in many other places. Please accept this along with our apologies for causing you this heartache. We are still here, although you can't see us all the time. When you do, it is real. [Sabrina said she still sees them all, out of the corner of her eye, often.] We will be around you for quite a while, until we need to prepare for our return. As you heal from this, we will slowly retreat, but you are so special that we can't entirely leave.

"We ask you to continue on your path. After enough time has passed, please take up with new children [goats]. We will be there to help you. Goats need a new way of living on this Earth, and you are one of the very few who agreed to this reworking of human values into a more compassionate and complete understanding of the value of life. There is a new way of Being available to us through the connection with you. We have been used as food and money but never in a partnership for mutual advantage. That is where we want to go. In partnership all things flourish, and everything becomes possible. *Nothing* is impossible. All dreams can come true, so please dream wonderful dreams of partnership with us. We can accommodate almost anything if asked and considered. We love you, Sabrina, and hope you come into remembrance of your true self, because then anything is possible."

The goats then requested, "Do not hurt the lion; just scare it away."

The lion herself had crossed a dangerous line in the killing of the four goats, because in the serial killing of these four, she found she enjoyed it. She returned several times over the following days after the killings, and a hunting permit was issued to allow for her to be shot on sight. The goats were adamant against this, so we all sent many messages out to the lion to stay away or she would be killed also. She must have heard and understood what would be waiting if she returned and was visibly trying to get more goats, because there was no more violence and, finally, no more tracks. I know she was concerned and confused about her choice to kill and the feelings it left her with, so I sent her thoughts of forgiveness and courage to believe in her better self and not get drawn into the darker side of her feelings. She left, completely gone to us, but her impact will never be forgotten.

Chemtrail Mix 2015
by Mary Tannheimer

I see the unmarked white planes on the tarmac being loaded with tanks. Then the tanks are being filled. Inside, the material is *forced* under pressure into the spray rigs for application. The elements of the material are jostling, bumping, and pushing each other as they are squeezed into a tighter and tighter space, finally crushed against one another until there is room for not even one more. They aren't supposed to be this close! They don't like each other, and *who* is making them be this close to each other? We *don't* like it! Let us out! You're crushing us all together!

Now the plane takes off, and they're flying. The bumping! Ow, oh, ugh! How much longer until we get out? Let us *out*! You're hurting us!

Finally the spray noise starts. Ow! *Noisy*! But we can feel the relief of those shot out who are flying *free*! Soon it's our turn. We're free! Agghh! We feel the sorrow of those who "died" in the tanks, left in the "schlogg" at the bottom. They "never made it out," which is sorrowing, but we *did*! Oh, so wonderful to be free and away from the pressure! Wheee, like children, the relief is so great! You're not touching me or pushing on me anymore! *We aren't supposed to be that close*!

Down they fall, speeding downward with no chute, spreading further and further apart and coming to their senses. They say, "Oh, what do we do now?" Spreading and spreading...look, there's more over there like us. Should we join them? We're not all the same, you know. Relief, such relief. Some of the trails are coalescing into larger, cloudlike structures. Choices are made. Some stay here, some go, some drop quickly, and some fly free, slowly moving down. Ah, *such* relief! Where to land? And then, "Who's down there?" Some pulled here, some there—like attracts like from the air to the ground. "Where will we go?" they ask.

There is a sense of reluctant duty for many; we do what we're told even if it makes us hurt. (Like the pilots of the planes say, "It's my job, and I have to do it.") Some enjoy the damage they cause—revenge for being crushed and spit out, injured inside and out—and seek like minds on the ground. Some recognize the error in allowing themselves to be used this way. (Nothing is powerless in full consciousness.) They seek ways to minimize the damage they do by slowing themselves down so they don't smack into things and penetrate so deeply when they stop, or they try to place distance between themselves as they fall (such relief) so the potency is diluted on arrival. They find like minds in the free fall and make groups to achieve their desired results. The floating and falling takes time, so they make their choices consciously. They ask, "Why do we let it happen to us?" Beliefs in victimization, lack of self-worth, mindlessness, revenge, hatred—these are not just human traits. These beliefs are projected outward and into all matter as is allowed. Consciousness learns at all levels and chooses the manner of its learning through the spread of experience. Thus is born Infinity, the infinity to choose.

"What do you believe that allows this to fall on you from the sky, unbidden (actually chosen), to damage the structures of your body and the world around you? Who do you dislike so much that you want to crush them to the bottom of the tank, lifeless and unfilled, to be thrown out on the ground and washed away? That is the reason this happens. It's a trail of violence leading directly back to you. How much do you hate yourself? We see where to go from high above and sort ourselves out to end our fall in the appropriate places. Some fall and cause havoc among the ones on *that* ground, because havoc is what those humans expect from life. Some fall and are blessed and forgiven, kissed with kindness and put to bed in the Earth to rest and recover from a difficult experience, because that is what the humans on *that* ground do with their lives—conscious examination and acceptance of difficulty in order to grow in wisdom.

"Love is the answer. Do you love yourself? Truly? Do you love others and allow them to grow? Truly? We live at the edge of reality, in the structures that bind and release at the most intimate levels of physical matter. We move through and are surrounded by the ether of God Consciousness, the *truth*, yet you affect us to such a degree that we can forget all of this and fall to your whims. You are *that* powerful! Imagine what you can do when you turn that power away from destruction and toward love. Imagine who you will be! *Imagine.* That is the word, for that's how it's done. Stretch into a new way of being, like clouds across the sky forming and changing into newness every second of their lives. Fly free in the current of love and see where it takes you. Soaring in the freedom of love is what life is all about, truly. Look up and recognize freedom. Your heart can go there and be blessed by the gentle rain of forgiveness and acceptance, to be spread on you and all around you. Reality begins and ends at the same place: Love. What's in the middle depends on you. The circle is never broken. You can ride it over and over, around and around until you understand the truth. Truly, love is the answer, and it is yours for *free*.

"There need to be places made that are blessed, that can call to these elements to let them rest and unbind from their distressing relationships. It won't take long. Soil tests can be done to monitor the potency of this unwinding in the ground (+ pH levels and so on), adjusted to limit contamination and aid in rebalancing. Technology exists to undo the divisive molecular bonding. Soul development needs to be pursued to undo the belief systems perpetrating the bonding. Harmonious relationships are possible, even with strong dissimilarity. There is a reason for difference. It's what makes each of us ourselves. Responsibility with Difference creates the Beauty of the Universe. It's there for us all."

Note from Mary Tannheimer: Use of the word *need* is a choice made in context of a smaller view of con-sciousness. Nothing actually "needs" to be done. It is all a choice, and choices made can create difficulty and distress or ease and beauty. It is ours to choose.

Ziggy the Cicada
by Mary Tannheimer

This conversation occurred on a walk above the KOA campground in Flagstaff, Arizona. Marianne and I had gone to a seminar in Sedona and were hiking during the morning of our last day in Flagstaff before returning home to Bishop, California. We had walked out the back gate on the grounds and gone along a trail that began to wind up the side of a mountain. It had poured rain the night before, and everything was glistening and clean, with beautiful smells in the air and a clear blue sky showing through the trees. We had walked for about fifteen minutes and were hearing cicada songs get louder and louder the higher we went on the trail. A bush was sticking out into the trail, and a lone cicada was perched on the edge of a branch at waist height, so it was easy to see by simply looking down. We stopped and looked at the big red eyes looking back at us, and we both felt this bug had something to say. We introduced ourselves and said we were writing a book about several topics having to do with human-nature relationships and would this be of interest to comment on. At first he seemed nervous with the contact, but as we were exclaiming how beautiful he was and what striking eyes he had, he seemed to puff up with pleasure and almost start preening with an exclamation of "Oooohhhhhh!" He said his group lives in the ground and had come out early because of all the rain soaking in. They were really happy to be out, he said. We asked him whether we could present some questions and whether he would answer them if he felt comfortable. He agreed, and so the following conversation ensued.

Mary: "What is the reason for the buzzing sound of your songs? It sounds like electricity."
Cicada: "It is electricity for the plants. We pull up energy for them from the surface and just below. The energy we use lays across the surface of the planet up to about three to four feet in height. Also, many of the plants' root zones exist in that surface layer, so we pull the energy up into the plants with the electric song and spread it around into the plants for vitality. Whichever insects are in the area respond to the call. The song calls them in to the electric field for the recharge."

We were quiet for a bit, and then the cicada went off on a different subject. He knew we were gathering information about how existing methods of relating to nature could be improved, and so he answered this question presented by Marianne.

Marianne: "What's up with the so-called infestation that happens in monoculture farmlands?"

Cicada: "We come into those fields in such large amounts because of the overpowering *yum-yum* smell caused by the lack of diversity in those fields. We can't help it. The singular smell overpowers us, and we have to come. If there were balanced diversity that humans cultivated, we wouldn't even be drawn to it; maybe only around the edges. The infestations by grasshoppers and other voracious eaters are more complex. They are being drawn in by the fear of people who are afraid of the infestations themselves. We try to show them their fear so they can understand it. Monoculture is an unbalanced phenomenon that does not exist naturally. Therefore, we insects do not behave naturally. Humans have large fears of lack of food, lack of water, and so on and can't see beyond this. They don't want to see that their own actions make these fears come to pass. We try to show them their fear, and they don't like us for it. It is part of our job to show people that they don't need to be this way. They reject us, they hate us, and they poison us."

When the cicada said this, he seemed to deflate and appeared disheartened. He then went on to another subject.

Cicada: "The chemical companies, the big ones, are trying to change the plants so that they can kill all of us when we eat the plants. This hidden group is keeping a large secret. They are trying to kill off natural plants and insects so they have control. This group wants only genetically engineered plants so that they can control the food supply and thus all the people."

I said we would be putting all this information in our book.

Cicada: "We knew someone was going to do it. I guess that's you."

We looked at each other and then at him.

Mary: "We will call you Ziggy. Is that OK?"

Cicada: "Mmmmmmm…"

He was done. He looked at us and then flew away. We looked at each other and said, "Wow, that was unexpected!" We sat for a bit and then continued hiking, each engrossed in our own thoughts. Quite a conversation from such a little guy. The smallest piece can be the most important.

Experimental GMO Corn Field and the Corn Maidens

On the drive from Bishop to Oakland, where I was going to do a construction job, I had gone through Yosemite (the quick route to the San Joaquin Valley) and was traveling along field after field of corn when I became aware that all the fields I was now seeing had warning signs posted. They read "Warning Do Not Enter—Experimental Field #7485, Experimental Field #8372," and were followed by the logo and name of a genetic engineering company on each sign. I pulled over to the side of the road and stared at the sign in front of me. "Warning…" I thought, *This is our food, and it's* experimental? *That could only mean one thing…All this corn is GMO? Every field? For miles? Aaaaaaaa!*

Here's another episode of *The X-Files:*

Corn Maidens (laughing, giggling, all crowding around): "The GMO process can't really affect the devas. They are too strong. It does cause weakness and discomfort (such as itching or nervous twitching and aches), kind of like the flu."

Corn Mother (steps forward): "Corn is an original plant brought here from another dimension, a global plant originally. It kept early peoples going."

Maidens: "They think they can take our souls, but they can't."

Mother: "Humans don't count. The GMO corporations don't care about you at all. You are like ants to them. It's all about power, about massive egos actually frightened deep inside, trying to feel worthy."

Corn Plants: "We are resilient. Their time is up, so they are frantic. The answer is in the sun. The energy is beamed through the sun, and we receive it. It makes us well. The GMOs can't take it and they fall away. The corn maidens throw the light and laughter, and we are nourished and sustained. Their mother (deva) provides us the solidity (strength, the base matrix) that underpins our existence, and her children provide the laughter and joy."

Mother: "Do not worry about what is to come. You two have made a great difference already. When you see an x-field, smile and acknowledge us, for we are behind it, even though we're unseen. We look for you and wait for your acknowledgement. Know we are there looking for your smile. It makes us strong in this dimension.

"Those that create these things on Earth are providing a service to humans who wish to believe in their own powerlessness and victimhood. Many choose this path and so need methods to perpetuate their existence in these beliefs. We would choose differently, or so we say, but we are not in human bodies on Earth at this time."

I received pictures of the beliefs while the last paragraph was being said. They were of anger, political protests, riots, junk food, GMOs, mugging, rape, dirty cities, noise, dead whales on beaches, piles of dirty plastic bottles, and so on. It was not a pleasant series of images.

Mother: "We will ultimately prevail, but you (humans) have much to learn about yourselves and others in this process of unveiling the truth about the foods you eat and what they actually are. They have poisons in them that actually latch on to your genetic structure and destroy it. They have toxins in them that addict you to themselves so you cannot resist the 'pull' of the poison. Therefore you seek it out. Resist the pull. Eat foods that are grown in integrity and truth, not in lying deceit. Bless all the food you eat and thank it for its sacrifice of life for your benefit. Even the most modified food will respond to this blessing and by this chathrough can be relieved. This kindness given by you will always have an effect in the larger picture, even though it is not readily apparent. Seemingly small actions have large effects in many dimensions, and they create change in a way that is not understood by many yet on your planet. You are all powerful creators, and change is your birthright. Be thoughtful and kind in your actions toward those life-forms that seem inert or unconscious, because consciousness is in all things, even the most innocuous, even the most common, whose existences you take for granted. You can create suffering or joy with a single word, a single thought, or a single look. Look at us, look at your food, and send us your love. Those of us who have been damaged by the fear of the scientists and the businessmen can be healed by your love, just as you can be healed by your love, even as you have been damaged by those same interests. They suffer much more than any of us ever will, because they suffer from fear, and that is the worst suffering of all. Help them, bless them, forgive them, but do not assist them in their ignorant ways. Create a new way for them through your own internal power, a way that says, 'We respect all life and will not treat it carelessly. It is time for you to do the same. We will have it this way now. It is the way of life, not death. It is the way of love, not fear. It is our way, and its time is now. Now. We will show you how it is done. You have nothing to fear. You have everything to gain, and you will gain the truth of who you are.' That is all for now, dear one. Keep us in your thoughts as we keep you in ours."

I sat awhile after this, looking at the corn blowing in the breeze. Like Mulder said, "The Truth is out there." I don't think he meant it in quite this way.

Gaia's New-Moon Message
November 29, 2016

Yes, I'm here, dear, and absolutely delighted to talk to you today. We're all gathered to give you a message—a song of hope—to get you through the coming times. Yes, things are chaotic right now. It's all bubbling to the surface to be seen, to be cleansed, and to be released from your reality. Underneath all this chaos is a deep quiet. That is the state I reside in, and at the center is peace. I welcome you to visit there often; it is in your heart.

I know it's hard to feel this peace and at times to even believe in it—for so many are in flux, in fear, in anger, in grief, and in pain. The pain is everywhere. But so is the love and the light. The light of day is shining through all the darkness, bringing out the dark intent, the lies, the manipulations, the corruption, and all that has prevailed for so long just under the surface. It's time to be seen and released.

My heart has remained steady at the center, always deeply devoted to you, my beloveds, my children of the Earth. The shroud of darkness has been so painful for me to see and feel. The bright light that is here now—surrounding us, filling us, cleansing us—is slowly but surely filling all those dark spaces with its brilliance. And I am overjoyed!

Although my physical body is different than yours and encompasses an entire spinning globe, my soul is the same. We're all here to experience, learn, and grow. And the journey has been painful at times for all of us.

I know, my child, it will take time, and the road isn't an easy one. It's winding and steep, full of potholes and rock slides and all manner of obstacles and challenges. But we're doing this together—all souls as one. Yet we each have our different paths to walk. We will all get there; of that I can assure you.

Continue to renew yourselves in my beauty as often as you can. Go to the mountains, the seashore, and the gardens. I will comfort you there. Share time with all my beloved animals, and love them in all their wondrous diversity. Let their ways fill you with joy! Scoop up the rich, dark Earth in a forest and breathe its aroma into your soul. Sit on a rock in the middle of a stream and let its song dance around you. Lay in the sand on a warm, sunny day and let the sun's rays caress you. Walk through a meadow and let the song of the flowers brighten your heart. And, finally, stand in the rain and let it wash you clean, drying yourself with rainbows.

I am with you always—in all ways. I cry with you. I laugh with you. I grow with you. And I love you.

What waits for us on the other side of all this turmoil is the beautiful world of our dreams. We are dreaming this world into reality together. Your heart, my heart, and all hearts. And it is beautiful.

Supplies and Resources

SOIL TESTS:

www.compostlab.net
  (local soil-testing laboratory in California)

www.ag.tennessee.edu
  (basic soil test for $7 per sample)

Soil-testing kits
  www.Gardeners.com/soiltestingkits

Peaceful Valley (soil tests, seeds, amendments, supplies)
  www.groworganic.com
  125 Clydesdale Ct.
  Grass Valley, CA 95945
  (530) 272-4769

SEEDS:

Pinetree Garden Seeds
  www.superseeds.com
  PO Box 300
  New Gloucester, ME 04260
  (207) 926-3400

Bountiful Gardens
  www.bountifulgardens.org
  10150 Foothill Blvd.
  Lakeview Terrace, CA 91342
  (818) 389-3864

Territorial Seed Company
   www.territorialseed.com
   20 Palmer Ave.
   Cottage Grove, OR 97424
   (541) 942-0510

Seeds of Change
   www.seedsofchange.com
   PO Box 4908
   Rancho Dominguez, CA 90220
   1 (888) 762-7333

Annie's Heirloom Seeds
   www.anniesheirloomseeds.com
   4646 Ransom St.
   Hudsonville, MI 49426
   1 (800) 313-9140

PLANTS:
Annie's Annuals and Perennials
   www.anniesannuals.com
   801 Chesley Ave.
   Richmond, CA 94801
   (510) 215-1326

FERTILIZERS AND AMENDMENTS:
Dr. Earth Inc.
   www.drearth.com
   PO Box 460
   Winters, CA 95694
   (707) 448-4676

E. B. Stone Organics
   www.ebstone.org
   PO Box 550
   Suisun, CA 94585
   (707) 426-2500

Whitney Farms
   www.whitneyfarms.com
   (866) 541-3114

Neptune's Harvest (fish/kelp fertilizer)
   www.neptunesharvest.com
   88 Commercial St.
   Gloucester, MA 01930
   (978) 281-1414

Fox Farm Soil & Fertilizer Company
   www.foxfarmfertilizer.com
   PO Box 787
   Arcata, CA 95518
   1 (800) 436-9327

TOOLS AND GARDENING SUPPLIES:
Compost Tumblers

   www.composttumblers.hayneedle.com

Northern Tool
   www.northerntool.com
   1 (800) 221-0516

Row cover hoops
    www.gardeners.com/rowcoverhoops
    Gardener's Supply Company
    128 Intervale Rd.
    Burlington, Vermont 05401
    1 (800) 876-5520

WALL O' WATER:

Wall O' Water Inc.
    www.wall-o-water.com
    PO Box 1379
    1480 Mt. Highway 91 North
    Dillon, MT 59725
    1 (866) 643-5036

FROST PROTECTION FABRIC:

    www.greenhousemegastore.com
    70 Eastgate Dr.
    Danville, IL 61834
    1 (888) 581-9337

HUMMINGBIRD FEEDERS:

Perky Pet
    www.birdfeeders.com
    (855) 737-5973

BEES:

The Hex Hive
    www.hexhive.com

Organic Beekeeping 101
　　www.organicbeekeeping101.com

ANIMAL COMMUNICATION:
Marta Williams
　　www.martawilliams.com

Carol Gurney
　　www.gurneyinstitute.com

Penelope Smith
　　www.animaltalk.net

RESOURCES:
Vermicomposting (composting with worms)
　　www.vermicomposting.com

The Farmers' Almanac
　　www.farmersalmanac.com

Quicksilver Productions (astrological calendars)
　　www.quicksilverproductions.com
　　PO Box 340
　　Ashland, OR 97520
　　(541) 482-5343

NRDC—Natural Resources Defense Council
　　www.nrdc.org

The Non-GMO Project
　　www.nongmoproject.org

Bach Flower Essences
www.bachflower.com
www.directlyfromnature.com
1 (800) 214-2850

Garden Rainbows Essences
www.gardenrainbows.com

FOOD SUPPLIES:
Vitamix Blenders
www.vitamix.com

Juicers
www.consumerreviews.com

Food Saver Seal-a-Meal
www.sealameal.com

Food Dehydrators
Best food dehydrators for 2016:
www.dehydratorjudge.com

Canning Site
www.simplycanning.com

EDUCATION:
Waldorf schools
www.waldorfeducation.org

These schools emphasize the role of imagination in learning, and they strive to holistically integrate the intellectual, practical, and artistic development of students. The aim is to inspire lifelong learning in all students and to enable them to fully develop their unique capacities. The arts are fully integrated into the teaching methodology. This inclusion in academia increases aptitude and creative thinking.

Inspired Parenting Magazine
   www.inspiredparentingmagazine.com

Their purpose is to inspire and empower families and children as well as to educate the hearts of families and children. If you're interested in learning more about your children's brilliant brains, tender hearts, sensitive souls, and courageous spirits as well as the myriad external factors that impact them on all levels, then this magazine is for you.

Wild Roots Forest School
   www.wildrootsschool.org

Wild Roots offers a curriculum rich in direct experiences with Nature that nurtures a sense of community and belonging among children, families, and the land. Wild Roots meets in local natural spaces, where the sky is the ceiling, the trees are the walls, and the floor is the living Earth. Their philosophy is that we're more likely to protect something we love and that to love it, we must know it. Natural settings give children direct experience with a world not made by humans, in which they can feel themselves a part of a larger community of life. Classes are offered in Santa Barbara, California, and Bishop, California. They are for young children, ages two and a half to six years old.

Books:
Worms Eat My Garbage
   May Appelhof

Let It Rot! The Gardener's Guide to Composting
   Stu Campbell

Behaving As If the God in All Life Mattered
   Machaelle Small Wright

The Findhorn Garden
The Findhorn Community

My Conversations with Animals I & II
Suzanne Ward

Earth Democracy
Vandana Shiva

I Can See Clearly Now
Mary Soliel

What Do You Mean the Third Dimension Is Going Away?
Jim Self and Roxane Burnett

Deep Truth
Gregg Braden

Charlotte's Web
E. B. White

SPIRITUAL RESOURCES:
Mastering Alchemy
Jim Self and Roxane Burnett
www.masteringalchemy.com

Alchemy is much more than the concept of changing lead into gold. Alchemy is a way of life, a pathway allowing you to step from your three-dimensional experience into a higher, more expansive awareness of life. They offer classes, free webinars, a monthly newsletter, books, and more.

In the Arms of Angels
    Jeanie Barnes, angelic channeler
    www.angelicchanneler.com

Jeanie is an angelic channeler, bringing messages from our guardian angels. The messages are delivered with love, offering support, guidance, and understanding from our angels.

Transformation through Reflection
    Ellae Elinwood
    www.songcarrier@gmail.com

Ellae offers personal readings and a monthly newsletter, "Mountain Musings." She is the author of several books. Her guidance is true and gets to the heart of the matter every time.

Laura Alden Kamm
    www.laurakamm.com

Laura is a spiritual teacher, speaker, and author in the fields of human consciousness, soul working, structural and medical intuition, mysticism, and personal empowerment. She offers classes and personal intuitive readings. Her readings are always delivered with pinpoint accuracy and always with the spirit of humor and love.

Joan and John Walker
    www.joanandjohnwalker.com

Discovering your true self *is* the key to freedom. Joan and John are spiritual teachers, and Joan is a gifted channel for the archangels and ascended masters. They offer classes, teleseminars, and conferences.

Mary Soliel
    www.marysoliel.com

Serving humanity through inspiring words and transmissions, Mary is a six-time award-winning author, channel of Archangel Michael, speaker, and gazer.

Suzy Miller
  www.suzy@suzymiller.com

To contact Suzy's assistant, Sharon Hall, e-mail her at Sharon@suzymiller.com.

Suzy is a former pediatric speech-language pathologist with a master's in education and a certificate of clinical competence. She is a pioneer in shifting the perception of autism, energetic sensitivities, and the experiences associated with new levels of human consciousness.

Suzy is the founder of the Awesomism Practitioner Process, educating parents and professionals around the world regarding the unseen gifts of our newest populations as well as how to use their gifts to gain greater personal self-awareness. She is the author of *Awesomism: A New Way to Understand the Diagnosis of Autism*.

ABOUT THE CONTRIBUTING AUTHOR

I was born in downtown LA and grew up and worked in LA and LA County. There I experienced art, music, theater, libraries, traffic jams, crime, the beach, dancing, family, friendship, bigotry, anxiety, love, mathematics, logic, machinery, disappointment, yoga, and animals. Then I left. I have lived in Bishop, California, since 1999. Here I have experienced sublime beauty beyond words, the uniqueness and difficulties of living in a small, rural town, friendship, love, fundamentalism of many kinds, the cowboy and Indian "wars" at the bars (still), economic collapse, the evisceration of the field of endeavor in which I have worked for thirty-two years, the growing into my own wisdom, and animals. I have also experienced working on this book with Marianne. This has been good for me. This life has been good for me, for I've grown.

You can contact me for one-on-one animal communication services as well as public-speaking engagements regarding animal communication.

Mary Tannheimer
m.k.tannheimer@gmail.com

ABOUT THE COVER DESIGN AND ILLUSTRATION ARTIST

I am fascinated with imagery, art, and color. This fascination began when I was a child and developed into an obsession that went from coloring books and comics to more refined attempts at art in high school. Next, I took my studies further into college. After earning a degree in fine art, I began my career as a professional artist. I paint large murals on buildings as well as commissions on canvas and outdoor scenes on location. I am always painting and drawing. I dream of making a significant contribution to the art world and hope for my artwork to keep developing toward that end.

Cover Art: Kevin Anderson
www.artmurals.us
artistkevinanderson@yahoo.com

Made in the USA
San Bernardino, CA
16 March 2019